To Pat,
with our love and prayers.

Blessings,

Celia & Mike.
xxx

To Have and To Hold

by
Mike and Celia Deakin

authorHOUSE®

AuthorHouse™ UK Ltd.
500 Avebury Boulevard
Central Milton Keynes, MK9 2BE
www.authorhouse.co.uk
Phone: 08001974150

© 2007 Mike and Celia Deakin. All rights reserved.

No part of this book may be reproduced, stored in a retrieval system, or transmitted by any means without the written permission of the author.

First published by AuthorHouse 9/19/2007

ISBN: 978-1-4343-1743-8 (sc)

Printed in the United States of America
Bloomington, Indiana

This book is printed on acid-free paper.

Acknowledgements

Bible quotations are from the New King James version (NKJ) Copyright © 1994 by Thomas Nelson, Inc. unless otherwise noted.

Other quotations are from The Living Bible (TLB), ©1971 Tyndale House Publishers, Wheaton, Ill.

Scriptures also quoted from The Message (™) copyright © by Eugene Peterson, 1993, 1994, 1995. Used by permission of NavPress Publishing Group.

For permission to use copyright material we are grateful to the following sources:

> AW Tozer "The Pursuit of God" Copyright © 1969 Christian Publications Inc. Harrisburg, PA, USA
>
> Quotations from The Word for Today by Permission from United Christian Broadcasters (UCB) Po Box 255, Stoke-on-Trent, ST4 8YY, England

- Tel: +44(0)845 6040401
- Email: ucb@ucb.co.uk
- Web: ucb.co.uk/wft
- Fax: 01782 764966

Free copies of this daily devotional are available upon request to UCB in the UK and Republic of Ireland.

Some of the names have been changed to protect the identity of others.

Contents

	Preface	ix
1	Mike's Story	1
2	Celia's Story	10
3	Hugh Christie School	19
4	An Angry Young Man	27
5	The Nurse Gains Her Wings	30
6	The Slippery Slope	35
7	Facing Reality	43
8	Mike Decides his Future	46
9	Celia – Back in the Army	51
10	Mike and Annette	56
11	Mike Joins the Army	60
12	A Brand New Start	68
13	Celia Arrives in Münster	76
14	Boy Meets Girl	82
15	A Time for Commitment	86
16	We've Only Just Begun	93
17	Just like being Born Again!	100
18	Back to Germany	107
19	The Move to Düsseldorf	116

20 A New Life in Nottingham 120
21 The One who is left Behind................................128
22 The Promise 136
23 Life with Pam 142
24 Celia Moving On 152
25 Family Life 157
26 A New Career? 162
27 The Times they are a'changin' 167
28 Mike Meets Penny..175
29 A Question of Faith..179
30 Phil's Surprise...181
31 Mike's Journey Back 187
32 The Year of 1999 190
33 Catching the Fire!..196
34 Spreading the Fire 203
35 Y2000 210
36 The Waiting Game 215
37 Mike Settles in Birmingham...............................220
38 The Post Dated Promise 223
39 Put in the Sickle, it's Harvest Time! 227
40 Gathering the Harvest in....................................233
    Celia's Prologue 245
    A Note on Restoration 248

Preface

When I was young I didn't understand the subtleties of life, the things that are obvious to an adult are hidden to the simplistic thoughts of a young child.

An immense pressure builds up; like a balloon when it is blown up to the bursting point, all of these images, good and bad, are being imprinted on our subconscious mind.

We often think that children aren't able to understand what's going on. However, behind their simple thoughts, there is a camera, video recorder; a sound reproduction system, that takes in every sound, thought or picture, to be re-lived at a later time.

Who knows what implications these will have on the future? These early years, are very often the deciding factor for later life. For how we will cope with everything that life hands us, marriage, children, relationships and so many other things.

Chapter 1

Mike's Story

This must be Paradise, I mused, as I lay on the beach under the Florida sun, wriggling my toes in the soft white sand. Celia, my wife and little Gracie, my Granddaughter are paddling in the sea, they turn and wave and I wave back.

In my minds eye, it was my daughter I could see, yet the memory was hazy. I had rarely seen my son or daughter during the last twenty years, a great void in all our lives! Yet, here they were beside me, along with a lovely daughter-in-law!

"Yes", I thought, "This is a holiday that should never have happened in the normal course of things! An impossible dream! But *a dream come true!*"

My mind began to wander. I thought back over those years, years that sometimes seemed to have been wasted. But, as I looked around with a sigh of deep contentment, I remembered that it was not always that way… How much has happened since then……

To Have and To Hold

* * ☙ * *

I was born, in Birmingham, England, one of twin boys, on Christmas morning, 1951. The Doctor would always remind me "I missed my Christmas dinner because of you, young man!"

Unfortunately, my twin did not survive. This was to have a significant effect on the family in the coming years, as my parents sought to replace the son they had lost.

This was the beginning of my journey into life. On the one hand I had two doting loving Grandparents, for whom I will be eternally grateful; the influence of their teaching in my life has had a significant effect, right up to the present day.

On the other, my Mum and Dad were married too young and probably for the wrong reasons. There were only two things that seemed important to them which really controlled their lives… work and booze.

My Father worked all day and most of the night, so in my formative years, my Grandmother was the one who taught me and was responsible for my upbringing.

She and Granddad were old school and believed in the old values, one of the legacies for me was that I was never allowed to speak slang or with the dreaded "Brummie" accent.

But I enjoyed going to Grandma's house. Life at Grandma's was easy going, as I learned the values that were passed on. These were to be the cornerstones of my life, as I grew up and faced the many challenges that were to come my way.

At the age of five and a half we moved as a family into a council Maisonette on the other side of town but I used to walk or cycle several times a week across the park to Grandma's.

Infant school was a blur and apart from falling over and being rushed to the hospital accompanied by a teacher; there wasn't a lot to remember. From what I do remember, school was an enjoyable experience and I looked forward to going each day to join up with the many other children of my age.

Junior school was a different matter. I loved school and everything to do with it. I was successful at all the academic subjects and excelled in Maths, English, Spelling and English Literature.

This enjoyment was soon cut short, the problem was, that being the firstborn and therefore the eldest child, I took on the responsibility for my two eldest sisters, from the age of seven. This, then became my role, for what seemed like an endless, ever-growing family.

Despite these interferences to normal school life, (more time away from school than attendances) I somehow managed to do well and passed the eleven plus exam to go to Grammar School.

Mum and Dad made it no secret that Mum always wanted to replace my twin brother, who had died a short time after birth. The problem was that five girls were born in quick succession, hence the steady growth of the family with seven children, with an average of one to two years between.

Life was hectic, what with getting up in the morning with Dad. Clearing the debris of the day before, making sure that Dad had a cup of tea and sandwich ready to go off to his days work. I then took tea to Mum who was still in bed. I had to make the beds and dress the kids, light the coal fire and feed whichever of five sisters was the baby. I then had to get myself ready for school and feed my pet dog Bruce who was the joy of my life.

In the evening, one or both of my parents would leave at 5.45pm to go and open the local pub. The other would follow later to serve behind the bar or stand at the bar.

Days off would mean bus or train journeys to Stourport or Bewdley or the High Street to make a pub crawl of every pub on the left and right of the street!

So by the time we reached our destination the alcoholic wheels were well and truly oiled. Many of the memories of that time were of feeling completely bored, because when we were outside the pub, the only time I could call my parents out, was if there was an emergency.

One vivid memory I have, is of standing with two of the kids in a pram outside a pub on the high street. I used to have to amuse my sisters while Mum and Dad were inside. One of the men came out and offered me a drink of beer… which I took. This process went on until closing time, each time one of the drinkers came out of the pub I was given another glass of beer.

When my parents came out, we started to walk with the pushchair to the bus stop. I was wandering about all over the place; I was drunk at seven and a half years old!

There was always plenty of booze at home especially during holidays. Christmas was one giant binge and inevitably ended up in a bad argument, turning to a fight. As I grew up the rows and fights became more regular and more violent.

Another memory I have is that I came home to hear Mum and Dad shouting and screaming at each other in the kitchen. When I tried to get in my father told me to go away but I could hear my mother screaming.

How I did it or where the strength came from I don't know! I managed to force the door and get in. All I could see was my Mum cowering in the corner, with my father towering over her with a frying pan or saucepan raised above his head. I stood between them and pushed Dad away. I think that the shock of that made him back off and put down the pan.

I stood looking up at him and remember the anger that was boiling up inside me. I said, "If you ever touch my mother again I'll kill you". I was between five and six years old at that time, the relationship between my father and I was strained or non-existent from that time on.

As I grew up, I became more and more responsible for my siblings and never really learned how to be a child. One of the bright lights at this time was that one day while I was out playing; a van came to invite any of the kids in the neighbourhood to go to the local church of England Sunday School.

From that, I joined the choir and was able to partake in an activity that has always been a love of my life – singing and music. I soon found that I had a talent, which gained the recognition of the Church. That brought about my second love which was to entertain other people. This was to become one of the things in my life which helped to offset the not so good things that were going on at home.

At eleven years old I passed the dreaded 11 plus exam with distinctions, which meant that I qualified to go to Grammar School. There was a sense of excitement at this, because we were always looked down on as a family, due to the obvious way of life that we lived. I had decided long ago that I would never be like my parents and maybe, just maybe, this would be the chance I needed.

As the time drew nearer, we went shopping to get all the uniform and sports kit that were needed to start at the Grammar School.

First day, as always, was a bit strange but I took no notice because there were a lot of new kids starting at the same time. I had no idea what to expect but as time moved on, it became obvious that the work routine and especially the homework, were going to be a challenge!

Having told of my life at home I leave the rest to your imagination, and then the bombshell hit! You see, all the kit I had was bought with vouchers from one particular store. So it soon became glaringly obvious that 'I was different' I also needed 'Free School Dinners' I was one of the poor kids!

I soon found that being different isn't easy and within eighteen months, I was behind, disliked, unhappy, bullied and missing time off school. School was very definitely one big chore and to be avoided at all costs. But of course it's not that easy!

To Have and To Hold

The truant officer was a regular caller while I was at home looking after my sisters. Eventually the "Powers that be" sent me, a thirteen-year-old kid, who had done nothing wrong, but try to survive, to a psychiatrist to check my mental state! No matter what he said there was no way I would rat on my family, to those who had now become, in my very jumbled mind, "The Enemy".

So, they decided to take me out of Grammar School and send me to the local comprehensive. News travels fast and by the time I arrived at the new school, every man and his dog had some version of the story as above. Just to encourage me further, the Deputy Head had also decided he knew the answer to my truancy, called me in and said that absence would result in the cane.

Things just went from bad to worse. I got sick and was off school. When I went back, the Deputy Head proved to be a man of his word. He called me to his office, with no discussion and gave me six strokes of the cane.

I was now labelled a trouble maker in his eyes and that of the other teachers. Isn't it amazing how so often we latch onto other people's opinions without finding out for ourselves?

The one subject in which I most wanted to succeed was Technical Drawing. But the teacher decided that because I did not learn as quickly as the others, he would give me a hard time. He constantly took the Mickey and told me I would never learn to draw. That little lie took another forty years to unravel.

"Just because someone can't do it right now doesn't mean they never can."

I managed to fulfil my desire to draw at the age of fifty, when someone took the time to show me, that I really had no problem with drawing, only incorrect information from a bully. The outcome of this patience was that I became a top flight kitchen designer!

"Don't let anyone steal your dream".

The end of this chapter in my life was that I left school illegally, never to return, at the tender age of fourteen.

Meanwhile, a quiet, shy young woman had just joined the British Army, with a dream in her heart to be a nurse.

Chapter 2

Celia's Story

I reached the Ticket Barrier at Canterbury Railway Station. "Tickets please. Tickets please". Now it was my turn. I had a huge Army case with me, "Where you off to, then?" he asked.

"Catterick" I replied.

"Oh, you don't want to go there! He exclaimed. "It's the back of beyond, full o' barracks as far as the eye can see!" "Cold, too in winter, blows in off the moors." He took my ticket, clipped it and handed it back to me, "Best o' luck! He smiled.

My Mum and Dad helped me across the station to wait for the train. We didn't have too long to wait, Dad lifted my case and kit bag aboard. I gave them both a hug and a kiss; I got on, found a seat and then waved to them as the train pulled away till they were out of sight.

I sat back to read my magazine, but I couldn't concentrate. At last I was on my way to my first Posting after Basic Training (Basic ARMY Training, that is!)

Yes, I had learned how to march, iron my white cotton poplin shirt (with detached collar and collar studs) till it was crisp, spotless and entirely crinkle free! I had learned the History of Military Nursing and all about Florence Nightingale, but now it was time to start being a real nurse!

As I sat on the train, I wondered if My Dad had felt the same when he left Canterbury for his first Posting to Penshurst.

* * 🐾 * *

It was 1940; the War in Europe had just begun. My Dad, George, had put his age up in order to join the army, he was actually only 16 years old and Penshurst, Kent, was his first posting, working on the switchboard. A friend of his was dating a girl who lived in the nearby town of Tonbridge. She worked at the Dowgate Printing Works, and was to be instrumental in bringing Betty, her work colleague and George (or Gluey) as he was known, together, by arranging a blind date!

George had spent the day on a route march with his unit and by all accounts the date was memorable, if only for the fact that they spent the evening walking the country lanes, so I imagine Dad's feet were pretty sore by the time they said goodnight at the railway station!

Later, Betty joined the Land Army, working in the fields around Lydd and Rye on Romney Marshes, not far from Dover. By all accounts it was hard work, not only that but they had to cycle to the fields along the country lanes, usually against a head wind, with Spitfires 'hedge - hopping' and Doodlebugs coming down all around them!

Meanwhile, George was sent to Southampton to join the flotilla of craft preparing for the great invasion which took place on D Day! He landed safely, and fought his way through France and Belgium to Germany, no easy task. He suffered nightmares for many years to come, and always slept with a peg wedged in the door to warn him if anyone tried to enter the room.

All through this time, they wrote to each other and when George managed to arrange some leave in August 1945, they hastily arranged a wedding! They enjoyed just a couple of days honeymoon in Ramsgate, before George was posted to Berlin to deal with some of the clerical work involved with the Potsdam Conference.

George came home in time for the BIG CHILL of 1947. The year which, because of the coal miners strike, coal was in short supply and the snow lasted from January to April, and then caused devastating flooding when it thawed. However, they must have found a way to keep warm, and I was one of the results!

Mike and Celia Deakin

* * 🐝 * *

I was born, Celia Marion Glew, in November 1947 in a Nursing Home in Tunbridge Wells, Kent. Housing in the south of England was in short supply after the war, as a result of the blitz. Mum and Dad were renting one room in which to live, wash nappies and cook on a single gas ring. They later moved to half a house, before being offered a new council house in April 1952.

George, no longer in the Regular Army, joined the Territorial Army, Military Police and in June was one of the soldiers who lined the route for the Coronation of Queen Elizabeth II. He remained "Army barmy" for the rest of his life! On 'Demob' he obtained a job as a Railways Clerk but was now working as a clerk at South Eastern Gas Board, in Pembury, just outside Tunbridge Wells and some 5 miles from our home in Tonbridge.

I started school in Tonbridge and quickly learned to read, which was to my advantage. I loved to read, sing and dance, a dreamy child who loved flowers and fairies and lived in a day dream world of my own. Having no brothers or sisters, I learned how to amuse myself.

My favourite pastime was to go to the local wood; it wasn't large now, because houses had been built on much of it! But I knew all the paths, every tree root to jump over! There used to be lots of primroses and bluebells but people had dug them up to grow in their own gardens, and I was sad about that, but it was still My Wood. I loved the atmosphere, the sense of being alone with nature, listening to the birds, watching the Spring turn into Summer, sitting in a moss covered clearing with the sun dappling through the trees.

Life was carefree then, we didn't have much, but then we didn't need much either! My Dad used to take me to school on the back of his motorbike, he dropped me off outside the Rose & Crown Hotel on Tonbridge High Street, and I walked through to The Slade School.

The Slade was a Church of England School, housed in an old building covered in Virginia creeper which turned wonderful shades of scarlet in the Autumn. It had two playgrounds, one for boys and one for girls, plus a grassy area edged with shrubs and flowering trees, which made great places to play. At dinnertime, after lunch we would be herded across the road so that we could play in the Castle Grounds, which gave us plenty of space to let off steam!

When I started at the Slade, I skipped the first year because I could read well, and because I was one of the oldest in my year. This meant that I spent two years with Miss Bentley, who was definitely a teacher of the 'old school'! She was very strict and probably quite frustrated at my inability to concentrate on the job in hand! She got cross because I rarely, if ever, finished a piece of work and my mental arithmetic was dismal. She knew I was bright and capable of much more than I was producing, so all my work bore the words "TOO SLOW" in red pen at the bottom.

My time keeping, when left to my own devices was not good either, though I was usually on time as a child because my parents made sure I was! But as I grew up, I was always late! My father and later on, my husband, both being military men, found this to be particularly irritating, and thought I did it on purpose.

For me it was dispiriting, and I ended up living up to what was expected of me. I was also 'stuck' with a nickname, thanks to my surname being Glew, I got called Gluey, Sticky and ol'Gluey she's all stuck up! So I retreated into my daydreams, and let criticism and rebuke wash over me like water off a ducks back! I guess it made me very resilient, which is quite useful at times, as I think without it I could have become oversensitive.

As a Church school, we had an Assembly each morning after Registration, when we prayed and sang hymns. There was always a piece of classical music playing as we entered and left the hall, a bible reading and a short message to inspire and encourage us to do our best. My form teacher in my third year was Mr King, who every week gave us a Scripture lesson, which I enjoyed. Our

School Motto was: "Manners Maketh Man" and we were taught to respect each other as well as our elders.

My Dad had always been 'Religious' and as a boy had been a choir boy in Canterbury. When I was 7 years old, he had an experience which changed all our lives.

The Parish Church in Tonbridge had been praying about the expanding housing estates in the north of the town. Their prayers were answered when a lady parishioner had donated her school building as she had now retired. The building was a wooden hut set on a brick base, with asbestos panels on the outside. This now required dismantling, moving to its new location and rebuilding on a new brick base.

For this task, the church enlisted the help of an international, ecumenical work party! They commenced each morning's work with a short time of worship around a large wooden cross, which they had erected on the site near our home. The group were quite a mixed bunch, including a Greek Orthodox Priest in all his regalia, which as you can imagine created quite a stir!

However, the most enduring impression which had a lasting effect on my dad was that of seeing a young American girl, sitting astride the roof in the pouring rain, (typical English summer weather) hammering in nails, singing choruses and praising Jesus at the top of her voice!

Thus began Dad's quest to find a real relationship with this Jesus who meant so much to this young girl!

Later, we began attending the little church and at a Parish Weekend, Dad, now a Christian, felt the call to full time ministry. Dad had got involved in the Sunday School which I had attended from the age of four, he ended up as Superintendent. He had also become the Secretary at the Church, which basically meant that he did everything except preach - and one Sunday he even had to do that, as the Curate didn't turn up to take the Service! Dad had just returned from an Army exercise weekend, and was still in uniform, but we had a church full of people, so that was Dad's debut as a Minister!

At the end of each school day, I had to get the bus back home. There were three of us who lived in the same area and we went home together, usually via the Castle Moat! No, not in it! But there was a path which ran alongside and in among the duckweed we could see water boatmen and damsel flies hovering above. There were also lots of grey squirrels in the trees and it was much more fun than walking along the road to the bus! The moat path brought us out by the river Medway, where we walked along between the river and the castle wall which towered to our left. At the foot of the wall, there were always flowers, Daffodils, or wallflowers, bright and cheerful!

To Have and To Hold

After a 15 minute bus ride, we walked along the road towards our homes but we often stopped to talk to the old road sweeper with his barrow. He seemed as old as old Father Time, but without the long white beard! We called him Poppidy-Grandidy! We always chatted to him and there was much laughter as jokes abounded!

Chapter 3

Hugh Christie School

My Mum had started a part-time job at the newly built Secondary Modern School near our home as a School Cleaner. This meant that she was at work when I got home but I didn't feel like a 'latch-key-kid' as there were friendly neighbours who would help if required. Usually, I would find something to occupy my time such as skipping, roller-skating or best of all working in the small patch I called my garden, until Mum came home, when I would set the table for tea. We would hear Dad's motorbike come round the corner behind our house and quickly put the cloth on the table ready to sit down to eat together.

My friend, Penny who lived opposite me would sometimes come over to play, she was brilliant at 'two ball' against the wall, but my co-ordination was such that I was painfully slow. We had always gone to Sunday School together, had been given identical dolls prams at

Christmas and later went to Bible class, Pathfinders and church youth club together.

During the school holidays, I would sometimes go up to the school to find Mum and amuse myself by drawing on the blackboard with all the coloured chalks! Penny had gone to the Grammar School the previous year. She was having to do Latin and seemed to have loads of homework! So I wasn't disappointed when I didn't pass my 11Plus exam, as I had already decided that I wanted to go to Hugh Christie.

So it was, that September 1959, found me starting a new phase of my life, only this time my classmates were mostly kids who lived on our estate, whereas before they had come from all over town. I also found that my cousin was in my class, and so we became much better acquainted. However, because I had not been at Junior school with the others, I was not quite accepted by them. My friend, from Slade School, now paired up with her 'best friend' who lived opposite her.

This I found was to be a pattern in my life, *my* best friend always seemed to have a *more preferred* best friend, so, as an only child I learned to make my own entertainment, my own opinions and my own way in life. This I later found to be to my advantage, as I was able to stand on my own two feet and not be swayed by popular opinion or trends.

I had by now graduated from Brownies to Guides, which were held at our church, where I gained my badges for Country Dancing, Child Nurse and Home Maker. At school, my best subjects were the more practical ones, Domestic Science (cookery), Needlework, and Music.

I enjoyed art, but was never given any instruction on how to achieve what I wanted. Our Art Master simply required us to "Paint me a picture", so those with natural talent were nurtured, whilst the rest of us were just left to our own devices. However, he did recognize a talent in me, that of sorting and tidying! His desk and equipment room became my responsibility to tidy every morning before school.

At the age of twelve, I was given my first bike for Christmas; it was a Hercules "New Yorker" in Electric blue. It was slightly too big for me and with a heavy frame and chrome mudguards, I was unable to ride it until the Autumn half term when it suddenly clicked and I was away! I had just learned to ride when I met Roger; one of Penny's admirers riding his bike around her house in the hope of seeing her!

I knew Penny wasn't keen on him, but he seemed a nice guy, we got chatting and rode around on our bikes together. During that week, we became good friends, though he still carried a flame for Penny, walking us to our bible class before going to the boys Bible Class held nearby.

After Christmas, Penny and I started going to Confirmation Classes and I suggested that he might join us. Penny was not impressed, but he did come along and I believe he made a commitment to Christ and became a keen member of the church youth club.

Celia aged 12

This was also a turning point for me; I made a decision to follow Christ, and as a result of a short stay in hospital decided that I wanted to become a nurse. I was Confirmed along with my Mum by the newly created Bishop of Tonbridge, who had been our Vicar until about a year before.

I wasn't a difficult teenager, but I remember being disappointed that I didn't become like an angel overnight, as a result of my decision. On the other hand I wondered why we repeated that we were "miserable sinners" in the General Confession, which was part of our Church service every Sunday, as I wasn't really aware of much wrong doing in my life.

This was about the time when Beatlemania erupted onto the music scene, and of course, we all sang and danced to our favourite songs before school started. Many of the girls, at 14 seemed quite grown up, but I was a late developer, so I didn't feel that I quite belonged.

However, I really enjoyed school, I had some wonderful teachers, including my Maths teacher, Miss Hayes, who helped me get over my dread of Maths (I was never any good at Mental Arithmetic at Junior School)! And Mr Howard was a fantastic Head Master! There was also an amazing character called Miss Geering, who taught Human Biology! She only stood about "four foot and a cornflake" tall, she had her hair scraped back in a bun and wore little round "owl like" glasses on the end of her nose. What she lacked in height, she made up for in shear exuberance and enthusiasm!

As a result of my decision to become a nurse, the Deputy Head Mistress, Miss Whitmore, recommended that I should aim at the State Enrolled Nurse (SEN) training, which only took 2 years and was a more practical course than the SRN (now RGN). She also arranged for

To Have and To Hold

me to skip the 3rd year and go straight into 5th year which would enable me to start on a Day release, Pre-nursing scheme.

This was a new course which had just been set up by the local Hospitals; I think there were about 10 of us drawn from the local schools. We all had to wear lemon coloured nylon overalls, so we were nicknamed "The Primrose Girls". I enjoyed the course and felt that I would enjoy nursing.

On my way home on the bus one day, I met the elder sister of one of my school friends. She asked me where I had been, and when I explained about the course, she showed me a brochure she had, about nursing in the Army. I knew nothing about it, but was very interested, as I had always wanted to go to Germany.

My father had shown me postcards of Berlin and talked about his time in Germany, about all the destruction and food shortages. I said then, (I was 8 or 9 years old) that I wanted to go to Germany, because I didn't believe all Germans were bad.

The other reason I thought seriously about joining up, was that my father, felt he should go to College to train for "The Ministry" and become a Vicar in the Church of England. This would mean moving away from Tonbridge, and I had no idea where Mum and Dad would end up.

If I trained in the Army, I would be entitled to free rail warrants, so I could get home….wherever that may be!

My subjects, that I sat for my exams were Maths, English, Religious Education, Human Biology and Needlework, I got a distinction for RE, and just about passed the others! Now, at fifteen and a half, it was time for me to leave school. I still remember, all of us 5th Year girls all standing at the back of the hall, sobbing because we were leaving!

So after a holiday job of picking Blackcurrants for two weeks, I started work properly, in the nearby village of Hadlow. I was working as a shop assistant in the village Chemist, balancing on a high rickety, step ladder in order to dust the dispensary and shop shelves, and serving customers. It was also quite lonely for me, working in Hadlow, as there was usually only, me and the elderly owner/dispensing Chemist and occasionally his wife, working in the shop.

I stayed there from August till January, when I decided that cycling the 5 miles along a dark country road was no longer an option. Then I managed to get a job at Boots the Chemist in Tonbridge, which I really enjoyed, as I made lots of friends with my new workmates.

Sometimes, my friend, Jenny, would come into the shop and suggest that we go to the Pictures, so we would book a day, but invariably found that it was a John Wayne film! I think we must have seen most of his films!

That first year, after leaving Hugh Christie School, I used to go back and join Miss Geering and my old class on my half day off, to study for my GCE Human Biology exam. I also went to a club which Miss Geering started, called The Old Christonians. It was a Christian club, but we did all kinds of things, like going on an archeological dig! I had already gained my Duke of Edinbugh's Bronze award, at school and now I was able to gain my Silver award.

Dad was now away at College in London, leaving Mum and I at home. I think that it was a time when we grew closer together, in understanding and love for each other. So, I felt a little guilty that I was applying to join the Army, leaving her on her own. However, I knew that they were pleased that I knew what I wanted to do, and Dad had the Army in his blood, so there was no problem, as far as he was concerned!

I passed all my fitness examinations and was accepted to join the Queen Alexandra's Royal Army Nursing Corps in June 1965. So, I said my farewells at work, and the Old Christonians gave me a good send off. My Mum took me to Tonbridge Railway station and waved me off, somewhat tearfully. I was on my way to Aldershot, which, as I later found out, is Home to the British Army!

Chapter 4

An Angry Young Man

During the next three years I worked in retail sales, whilst trying to find out who I was and most of the time going in the wrong direction.

One of the things I found out was that I revelled in one-to-one contact with other people. This was to have a major effect later in life, but at seventeen I was an angry young man, not having any real direction or even any ambition.

Unfortunately I started to work in a pub (now there's a surprise)! Starting work at 8am finishing at 2am the next morning, the die was cast.

I saved up and got my first motorbike which I loved because of the freedom it gave me. I had learned to drink in heavy bouts from early on in my life but now it became serious. I got in with the wrong crowd (Hells Angels) and spent more and more time just ahead of the law.

A significant moment in my life was just about to happen. As usual, I had gone to the local meeting place and was sitting drinking, when one of the angels came in all in a fluster. "The skins are coming" he shouted.

We went up on our bikes to warn the other guys who were at the fun fair at the top of the town. We found them and everyone got back on the bikes. On the way back the Police stopped the traffic to let us through. They knew that although there was going to be trouble, the local angels were not likely to be the instigators.

I was chosen to go and see if they, the enemy were coming. By the time I came back, the skinheads had come in another way.

Looking back, I can see that the only reason I was in this situation, was that I was accepted for who I was, no questions asked. I can now see, that although I wouldn't have admitted it then, I was scared out of my wits, I knew that literally anything could happen in the next hour!

But by now the adrenalin was flowing, so I jumped into the back of a small Ford van and we drove onto the adjoining car park which would turn out to be the battle ground and for me the place for a reality check! Bikes, Scooters and people were making a horrendous noise. My heart was beating so hard that I thought it would come out through my chest

All of a sudden KABOOM – KABOOM! It sounded like we were inside a drum! One of the angels at the back of the van kicked open the rear doors and said "the xxxxx's have got a shotgun, let's get out!'

At that moment, finally, I decided to use some common sense. I was very close to getting killed or at the least severely injured. I decided that it wasn't a good idea! I shot out of the back of the van, headed for my bike and drove off with no glance behind me.

By the time I was on the main road, my body had just about caught up with me. On the way home I decided that I needed to do something with my life, but what?

Chapter 5

The Nurse Gains Her Wings

I was standing on Waterloo Station when a somewhat nervous young woman approached me, "Are you going to Aldershot?" she asked.

"Yes, I am", I replied. "Er….are you joining the QA's?" she stuttered. I smiled and said "Yes, as a matter of fact, I am." "Oh, thank goodness", she sighed. I could see the relief all over her face, "Come on; let's find the train together, shall we? I said.

"Oh, by the way, my name's Celia, what's yours?" "I'm Daphne", she panted as she heaved her suitcase onto the train.

We were in a carriage that had no connecting corridor, (which was a peculiarity of London commuter trains, then) when I saw a girl pass our carriage along the platform. She was dressed in black, but had a halo of beautiful, strawberry blonde hair. I ran onto the platform and shouted after her "Hello! Excuse me!! Hello?"

Mike and Celia Deakin

She turned around, recognised me, and started walking back! I had met her, briefly, at the Army Careers Office in Chatham, where we both signed on together. She joined us in our carriage, introducing herself as Lynne. We didn't know it then, but we were to spend the next three and a half years together, and *they* became best friends.

We were all seventeen and a half years old, and were not old enough to commence our nursing training, so we stayed in the Basic training camp for the next six months. When we arrived we went through all the Army's procedures, which included blood tests. For this the MO decided that the place where most blood was to be found was….the earlobe! As Daphne later described the event to our Sister Tutor, "Yeah, they pierced yer earlobe and then yanked on it for yonks!!" Sister Tutor did not understand the terminology and was definitely NOT AMUSED!

Following on in time held tradition, the Senior Squad came to pay us a visit. They treated us to a graphic illustration of the weekly event known as "Pay Parade". Unfortunately, this has long since passed, with the advent of new Banking Practice, but afforded *us* much merriment!

So, also did the kit issued to us! Until our NO1 and No2 dress uniforms had been tailored, (two styles of skirt and jacket suits) we had to wear our PE kit. This consisted of a BRIGHT red aertex shirt, a grey flannel "A" line skirt, (which almost reached your knees) and the biggest grey, bloomers you ever saw!!! They were, of course, nicknamed "Passion Killers" and as we were sent each week on a cross country run around Aldershot, wearing said PE kit, as you can imagine, the spectacle was not a pretty one! That was obviously the idea, but it was also obvious that we could be seen for miles in these red tops! However, that never stopped us from running hopefully past the Para Barracks!!

Nor did it stop us from jogging very gently, not to say, walking, along the canal tow path, where we knew we couldn't be seen. Which ever way we came back to the camp it was uphill, so by the time we had run a little up the hill and through the gate, we always looked as if we'd run all the way!!

My Dad had now completed his college course and had been offered a Curacy at a Church in Canterbury. This entailed them moving house, so when I went home, I went to Canterbury for his Ordination. I never went back to Tonbridge to visit friends and so we lost touch. It was 30 years later before someone decided to have a School Reunion, and I have only kept in touch with two people since then, one being my Maths teacher, who, as I discovered all these years later, is also Celia.

In October, after some home leave, we were posted to Catterick in North Yorkshire. We met at Kings Cross

Mike and Celia Deakin

Station, only to find Daphne in a flap because she had left her Gas Mask at home! Since Britain was at peace at the time, we assured her that she would be fine until her mum could post it to her!

On arrival, we were allocated to a ward to work for a month, until our Course started. I was put on Children's ward. I still remember one of my patients, her name was Tracy and she had been born with Hydrocephalous - water on the brain. She was about 8 months old; her head was so large it had to be turned every 2 hours. She could not communicate, but I loved her, and when I went in to feed her or wash her I would sing to her and pray for her. One day, I will see her in the arms of Jesus.

Catterick certainly lived up to its reputation, that Christmas, we had nearly 2 feet of snow, but I was unprepared for the warm welcome I received at the Sandes Soldiers Home. Sandes was started in Ireland, about 100 years before, by a Miss Sandes, who took pity on lonely soldiers and wished to offer them a Home-from-home, where they could relax, write letters home and also hear the Gospel, the good news about Jesus love for them.

I was welcomed into a warm and loving fellowship of believers. I had been aware, when I first joined the Army, that I would need to boldly stand up for my faith in Jesus but it wasn't always easy to stand alone. Now I had Christian friends, mostly male, but I found that I was accepted as one of them and we spent many hours together. One of the guys, Tony, I really fell for, but he was older than me and though he was kind he didn't return my feelings, first love is always hard to bear, while it lasts.

However, I flourished as a Christian, in such an environment, my faith grew visibly. I was introduced to SASRA… The Soldiers' and Airmen's' Scripture Readers Association and became a Serving Member. SASRA has full time and part-time men and women who are basically missionaries to serving members of the Forces. They often work alongside the Chaplains and also seek to encourage Christians to meet together, and to actively share their faith with those they live and work with.

Chapter 6

The Slippery Slope

In the summer of 1966, I watched England win the World Cup, whilst home on Embarkation Leave, prior to going to Cyprus.

I arrived in Cyprus in August, having never flown before, (it was a 7 hour flight, then!) to the burning heat of the tarmac… and it was only 6am! We had seen from the plane, the glittering sea and the "pearl necklace" of tiny clouds that often ringed the Island, it was so beautiful!

I wasn't sure how I would cope with the heat, with fair skin and blue eyes, I knew that I burned quite easily and had also suffered Prickly Heat. Well, when we arrived at the Hospital, we were all put on Night Duty for the first week, which was a stroke of genius, as we were able to sleep through the heat of the day and work at night.

However, at the end of the week, we all went down to the beach and….. I got burned! I think I burned 3 or 4 times in the 16 months I was out there, until I finally built up something like a tan. Of course, sunburn

To Have and To Hold

was considered a Self Inflicted Injury, so it was no use complaining about it, or you might be put on a Charge.

Wherever, I went around the camp, it seemed the sound of the Beach Boys with Good Vibrations seemed to be heard. Isn't it funny, how even the opening bars of a certain song have the power to transport you back to a time and place; even now I find I can remember places with crystal clarity, seeing myself walking down a particular road or sitting in a café.

Yes, I loved music and I loved dancing and I enjoyed male company. So, it was inevitable that with little else to do in the evenings, I was drawn like a moth to the candle flame. "The Waggoner's" was the name of the NAAFI club at the Royal Corps of Transport, down the road and they had a Dance on every Wednesday Evening.

I wasn't interested in drinking, like some of the girls, I just wanted to dance. Invariably the guys would emerge from the woodwork just before the end, in the hopes of walking you home. Anyone would have thought they had done you some great favour, because on reaching the gate of the compound, they would suddenly change into a great hungry monster. I found myself having to fight them off, as they tried to go beyond the bounds of respectability.

Cyprus, at that time was full of troops of several nationalities, all serving with the United Nations Peace

Keeping Force. So it was that we received an invitation to a Dinner and Dance at the Danish Sergeants' Mess, in Nicosia. These were held about every 6 weeks, and were fantastic occasions. In the winter, the meal and dance were indoors by candle light but in the summer, they made the most of the balmy air and set up tables in the garden, with a dance floor and lights hung from the trees.

We found the Danes to be friendly, courteous, funny, and great company! Unfortunately, we were like Cinderella and had to be back in Camp by Midnight. For one of these occasions, my friend and I booked ourselves into a hotel in Nicosia, so we wouldn't have to come home with the others. We stayed on at the party till dawn, when they decided to lay the tables outside for breakfast. It was wonderful!

On another occasion, we waited for the Danish minibus to arrive, and discovered about four Swedish guys already inside. They all, Danes and Swedes looked somewhat sheepish!! Apparently, our Danish friends had heard about a Swedish Hospital in Famagusta, and thought it would be great to invite some Swedish nurses along. What they didn't realise was, they only had male nurses at Famagusta!!! So they were somewhat disappointed!

We actually did a sketch at Christmas, called Cinderella, based on the story of a nurse out with her Swedish Boyfriend, who looses her late night pass. I played the part of the Personnel Officer

Part of the Swedish Contingent was also based in Larnaca, which was our nearest town. We were often in Larnaca and so we met quite a few of the Swedish lads around the town. I was always amazed at how easily they tanned, you'd think that they would burn, being so blond and blue eyed. Instead they looked like Greek gods, so tall and handsome. They were also polite, gentle, amusing and sensitive.

I was smitten with one in particular, who was nicknamed Esso, whom I went out with for some time, until his 6 month stint came to an end and he returned to Sweden. I tried writing to him in very broken Swedish, using an old dictionary which one of the guys gave me, but he only knew how to write very formal letters, so I would read, "Dear Miss Glew", it wasn't exactly what I had wanted to hear. I have often thought about him over the years, and prayed for him to find Jesus.

It wasn't that there weren't any Christians in Cyprus, but at that time I just wanted to do my own thing. I knew that one day, I would return to the Lord Jesus, but not now. I knew that he still loved me and I'm sure He kept me from the worst excesses!

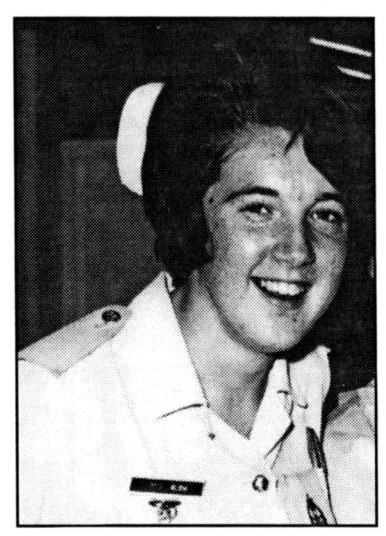

Celia in Cyprus

In the Autumn of 1967, it was decided by the powers that be, that since it should only take 2 years to do the SEN nursing course, they would have to send us home to UK early, since we had done 8 months before we went to Cyprus, which was supposedly a 2 year posting. We also still had to do 3 months Geriatric nursing at a civilian hospital, since it was rare that we ever nursed anyone over 50, let alone the elderly!

So, we arrived home in late November, with 5 weeks disembarkation leave, I didn't have to report to my new posting till January 2nd 1968.

I arrived in Tidworth in Hampshire, on Salisbury Plain to a bleak winter landscape. Although it was many miles south of Catterick, it had similar wide open rolling hills, and a lazy wind that blew straight through you!

In February, we were seconded to The Lord Mayor Trelore Hospital, in Alton, Hampshire. We quickly found that, Geriatric Nursing was very hard, yet the patients (with one notable exception) were *so* appreciative.

Soon, it was May, and we were back in Tidworth, just in time for our Final Exams in June. There was no big deal about this, as we had already passed harder Army Nursing exams, but these were mainly of a practical nature, which had the potential to be somewhat nerve wracking! However, I don't remember being nervous and we all passed and duly qualified as State Enrolled Nurses (SEN's).

I was going out with a lad called Chas, who was in the Royal Military Police (RMP). Their Mess was not too far from the hospital, and was quite small and friendly, whereas the hospital NAAFI was large and sometimes rowdy.

I liked Chas, he was a nice guy, but that was as far as it went, really. I even invited him to visit me at home, in Canterbury, when we were on leave. He was the first boy I had ever taken home, but my Dad was not impressed; he was Roman Catholic and his dad owned a Pub in London, so that counted him out of the reckoning!

Mike and Celia Deakin

Dawn

Slowly, so slowly, the night slips by
I sit here thinking, wondering why
Love is denied me. Is love so shy?
The one I love can never be mine
His kiss a taste of bitter-sweet wine
How can I stop myself from cryin'?

Darker now is the sky before dawn
Birds are stirring to welcome the morn
Yet still I sit here alone and forlorn.
But wait! The sky is growing light!
Clouds are glowing pink, gold and bright
Gone are the shadows! Gone is the night!

The sun brings hope to my heart again.
Like flowers bloom after falling rain,
Gently soothing my cares and pain.
Someday I'll find a love that is new
Someone somewhere whose love will be true
Then I'll forget that love once was blue.

Written by Celia in Tidworth, August 1968

To Have and To Hold

I was now 20 and due to come out of the Army in November, so it was decision time. What should I do? I thought about finding a job in Bristol, where my friend came from, but wasn't sure. So, having no real leading in any direction, I decided to go back home. My Mum and Dad drove up from Canterbury to collect me and all my stuff, they arrived on Wednesday, and I took them along to the SASRA meeting that evening, which they enjoyed.

The next day, I loaded up their car with all my bits and pieces, and said, "I'll come home by train, tomorrow, as the boys at the RMP's Mess are having a farewell party for me". "Don't worry about me I'll be fine!" I won't tell you what they said, but you can imagine that they were not too happy!!

Well, I enjoyed the party, said all my farewells, (Chris and I were just friends by this time), and the next morning set off down the road to the bus stop. A Landrover roared past me, screeched to a stop, reversed and one of the RMP's leaned out of the window, "Hi there, want a lift to the Station?" "Oh, yes please," I said, jumping in beside him.

We chatted away, and then they stopped in at their regular café on the way, where they treated me to a coffee. Then we carried on to Andover Station in good time for my train. So you could say, I was escorted to the Station by the RMP's, but they don't usually wave cheerily as they leave, the way they did to me!!

Chapter 7

Facing Reality

After helping out in the local Christian Bookshop for four weeks, I started working at the Kent and Canterbury Hospital. I had asked for Orthopaedic ward and found that women's Ortho was very different from the Men's ward next door! Instead of young men with sports or motorcycle injuries, it was full of elderly women with fractured hips or coming in for hip replacement operations. It was hard work and although it was a new ward, and well laid out, there were miles of corridor between one part and another. Whoever designed it didn't consider the poor nurse's feet!

I moved to Private Wards, which I enjoyed and gained much valuable experience. I can still see the Ward Sister, quite a larger than life personality, steaming down the corridor like a Galleon in full sail!

In May, my Mum and Dad moved to Christ Church in Ashford, Kent. So I moved with them and got a job at Willesborough Hospital. I worked first on Maternity ward then on Intensive Care, where I took a 3 month course in Coronary Care.

Living at home with my parents was now quite difficult. I felt that my wings had been clipped. I could no longer come and go as I pleased, if I went into town, shopping, Mum expected me home for dinner, and got upset if I didn't show.

I was also going through a major guilt trip, spending so much time on my own, I had plenty of time to recall in minute detail, all that I had done. The remembrances caused me much grief, and I began to seek for a deeper meaning to my life. I knew that God forgave sins, but somehow, I didn't feel forgiven.

At an after church group, I sought counsel from a Christian couple, who suggested I read "The Pursuit of God" by AW Tozer. This was what I read, and prayed.

"The man who has God for his treasure has all things in One. Many ordinary treasures may be denied him, or if he is allowed to have them, the enjoyment of them will be so tempered that they will never be necessary to his happiness."

"O God, I have tasted Thy goodness, and it has both satisfied me and made me thirsty for more. I am painfully conscious of my need of further grace. I am ashamed of my lack of desire. O God, the Triune God, I want to want Thee; I long to be filled with longing; I thirst to be made

more thirsty still. Show me Thy glory, I pray Thee, so that I may know Thee indeed. Begin in mercy a new work of love within me. Say to my soul, "Rise up, my love, my fair one, and come away." Then give me grace to rise and follow Thee up from this misty lowland where I have wandered so long.

In Jesus' Name, Amen.

So, I started my own Pursuit of God. Before this He had always been there in the background, but I had not really taken a lot of notice of Him. Now I needed some answers and I wanted to find Him.

It seems that there are keys which turn heavenly locks, and I believe this was one. As I took my decision to pursue after God, He set the wheels of my future turning in the heart of a young man in Birmingham.

Chapter 8

Mike Decides his Future

The next day when I woke up the activities of the previous night were very much on my mind. The possibilities of what could have happened seemed to be etched in glorious Technicolor.

One thing was certain; I couldn't go back and continue with that lifestyle. The obvious consequences of the life I had been living, were, that at the least, I could get into serious trouble, maybe even going to jail.

I felt that I had no one to talk it over with, least of all my parents. At that moment I suddenly felt helpless and very lonely. I couldn't get my head around the helplessness of my situation. What should I do? What was the next step?

The future seemed suddenly a wide open cavern, waiting to swallow me up. Everything from the last few years seemed suddenly, to envelop me, what do I do next? Where can I go? How can I make sense of it all?

When I was 12 years old I had found a place of refuge, it was the first time I had been allowed to go out on my own. I can't remember what the occasion was but at that time it had given me a sense of freedom that I had not known before.

With no sisters with me, I was as free as a bird! I went into the city centre and having found the science museum I wandered in. I was inspired by all the wonders, natural, and man made.

So, it was to that same place of solace that I now headed, but no matter how much I tried to think it out, I couldn't get any peace.

When I came out of the Museum I wandered aimlessly, not knowing where I was going or indeed why; then suddenly there it was! It just seemed to leap out at me! The answer!!

* * 🝯 * *

During the last few weeks, every time I had switched on the TV, there had been an advert for joining the Armed Forces. Somehow, it had lodged in my subconscious and now, here I was, facing the Army careers information office! I really wasn't dressed to go for an interview, but what the heck, what had I got to lose?

The officer I spoke with had an officious tone but I realised that this was what the forces was all about.

To Have and To Hold

Once I had come to terms with that, I found he was willing to give me his time, to find out who I was and where I came from. He really listened to me and in a strange way I liked his no nonsense approach, which in some ways reminded me of the way my Grandma had spoken to me in my early life

I had no problem with the exams so the next thing was my medical. A week later I came out feeling very satisfied. I went straight home that night and spent the rest of the evening thinking of all the things that would happen in the near future. The only negatives I could find were that I couldn't swim and how was I to tell my parents.

In the end, I decided that it would be best to tackle the subject in the morning, when they would both in a better frame of mind and sober.

They say that the best laid plans of mice and men falter, well this was one of those times. My father came in as usual at around midnight and went through the ritual of stumbling from bedroom door to bedroom door to check that we were all in bed.

When he noticed that I was awake, he came in, so I said, "There's something that I need to talk about to you and mum".

"What's it all about?" he said

"I'll talk to you in the morning" I said

"Give me a clue," says he

"Oh, what the heck!" I think, "I'm joining the army."

His reply, "Which girl have you got in trouble?"

There was only one girl that had been of interest to me and he knew that, her name was Annette but that's a later story.

The next day, I told my mum, who was definitely not happy, but I had made up my mind to take control of my own life, I was going to start planning my future.

The first thing I did was sign on as unemployed. I had been sacked the week before from a factory job on piecework. I had hated the work, which made me feel like a worthless robot. But that's the only job you can get when you are seen as thick, because you have no formal qualifications.

What rubbish we feed into our young people, when everything about our ability, is measured by what someone thinks about us, written on a piece of paper.

Then I went to the swimming baths to learn how not to sink in the water! This was the first time since I had been at school, where I had been bullied and ducked because I couldn't get the hang of swimming.

I went every day and learned basic crawl, by swimming very gingerly across the corner of the baths.

To Have and To Hold

After six weeks of faithfully going and learning, one stroke at a time, I conquered, in a fashion, the fear and perceived inability, which I had about swimming. For the first time that I could remember I felt a real surge of pride at this enormous achievement, by overcoming one of my mountains.

Two negatives dealt with! We can achieve the seemingly impossible if our reasons are big enough.

I was getting really excited as each day passed. The days just seemed to fly by! One week I took my medical, then trade interviews, medical results, I was accepted and ready to go! Suddenly, I had a purpose, no one was going to change my mind or sour my opinion of what I was about to do.

"This is it!" Off to the train station. Mom in tow, getting all upset. I didn't like that, I felt uncomfortable around people who were crying, or sad in any way. You know, Men don't cry! I had hardened myself against any show of sentiment, couldn't wait to get on the train. Made an excuse to get on as early as possible, leaving Mom on the platform.

At last! The train pulls out, one last wave and I'm free.

Chapter 9

Celia – Back in the Army

I had decided that my life lacked challenge and direction, so I decided to join the QA's once more. I rejoined in July 1970 as a Lance Corporal, and my first posting was in Woolwich, London. I enjoyed my time there, as it was close to home and even closer to London, so was great for shopping, or going to Shows and events.

Whilst I was at the Royal Herbert Hospital in Woolwich, I took a six month course in Orthopaedics. We had two large wards of Men's Ortho, two theatre lists a week and a very high standard of care.

Night duty in the Army was always done on an Internal Rota System and the usual night duty stint was 12 hours per night, 8 till 8, working 7 nights, then 7 off. At RHH, however, we were expected to work 14 nights followed by 7 off, then back on day duty.

Patients' who had been operated on were sent home on sick leave to recuperate. They had to return on Sunday evening, no big deal, you may think, but we often had up to 20 - 30 guys arriving! We had to find their notes and x-rays, and if they had plasters on, these had to be cut down both sides and then bound together again with bandages, in order to be seen by the Surgeon on Monday morning! So, that was fun!

Some would have to stay for intensive Physio, whilst others would be discharged to their Units. So, we usually had some "Walking Wounded" in Ward 2, whilst Ward 1 was for those having Operations. Monday's and Thursday's, we prepared patients for Theatre whilst Tuesday's and Friday's were always busy as we dealt with the Post Op's! So, by the time we had worked 14 nights like that on the trot, (there were just 2 of us on Night's) you can imagine we were pretty drained!

I completed my Course in June 1971 and was soon Posted to Iserlohn, in West Germany. I flew into Düsseldorf Airport arriving late in the evening; I was shown to my room and went to sleep. When I awoke in the morning, I was delighted to look out of my window to see a large weeping willow and a hill covered in trees!

Iserlohn is an attractive small town near Dortmund, in what is known as the Saureland, a green Isle in the middle of Germany, all trunk routes by-pass it as though none should disturb its solitude! Land of a thousand hills, a thousand wells, the land of caves, of slate, of forests and of dams! Yes, this was the area made famous by The Dambusters!

The town itself was dominated by a huge department store called Karstadt, which was lovely to shop in, but added nothing to the character of the town, flanked, as it was, by a large square, beneath which was a ground level car park! On the opposite side of the square was a modern building, The Dresdener Bank. It wasn't quite what I had expected!

However, further investigation revealed some interesting back streets, the Town Hall (Rathaus), and a large church. Apparently, Iser means iron, and Lohn means forest. Iron ore and zinc carbonate was mined here, and many wire products were manufactured in the town, making the town quite wealthy, however, there was the constant hazard of fire, due to the numerous forge chimneys. The town burnt down entirely seven times, the last occasion being in 1712, after which many beautiful stone houses were built, which are still well preserved.

However, within five minutes walking distance from the Hospital was a lake called the Seilersee, which you could walk around, and the hill I could see from my room had paths to the top where there was the (almost obligatory) Turm or tower. These I found, were built on most hills, and were the focus of the Sunday afternoon stroll, *so* enjoyed by every German family!

To Have and To Hold

* * Ⓥ * *

Often there weren't many Christians around the Military Base, but in Iserlohn, I found a few and we met together once a week for Bible study, and saw one another around the hospital or in the dining room. It was in this somewhat artificial atmosphere of being thrown together with a handful of people who you think you have something in common with, that I met Simon.

I was beginning to think about settling down, but didn't really have the opportunity to mix with many men of like mind. The chance comment of a well-meaning Christian lady sowed a seed in both our minds. He proposed, I was flattered and accepted. We began making plans and suddenly I was caught up with the romance of "marriage" and "weddings".

We went to my parents' house for Christmas, and I suddenly discovered that I was not at all sure that I wanted to spend an hour in his company, let alone a lifetime! However, we survived the holiday, but when he'd gone, I confided my fears to Mum.

Before I came home on leave, Deputy Matron had called me into her office to ask if I would consider moving to Münster, as they were short staffed. I told Mum I would take her up on her offer, as it would give me space to consider my options.

I arrived back in Iserlohn on New Year's Eve, went to see Deputy Matron and told her my decision. I was to leave for Münster the following afternoon! So, I went to my room and packed my bags, went to the New Year's party to say my farewells and fell into bed.

It had been a long day, I had no way of contacting Simon but even if I could, I wanted to go before he tried to change my mind. We missed each other by about an hour as I left on the minibus for Münster, I knew he would not be pleased but now my life was going in a new direction.

Chapter 10

Mike and Annette

Sitting on the train, I had a chance to gather some of my thoughts together. I realized that I hadn't got a clue what this adventure held in store. So I did what most people do when faced with an unknown situation, I sat there and prayed.

Me, whose life was totally opposite to all I had learned about God, a drunken, adulterer, foul mouthed, heartless and general 'layabout'; I prayed! The most amazing thing was, I believed he had heard and answered my prayers! Having spoken to many people since it seems that I was not unique in this experience.

Sitting there, the uncertainty began to dissolve, a strange sort of peace. It reminded me of when I was in the choir; I had always got to the church early, before anyone else had arrived, I had just stood in the church, in peace.

My mind was now free to think clearly and to recall some of the better, sweeter days.

Mike and Celia Deakin

I started to think of my lovely Annette, she was the one and only light of my life.

We had first met while I was working behind the bar, when I was about eighteen years old. One of my drinking partners, turned out to be her husband, but when I met her, I was not aware of that.

This night he came in as usual, but with this beautiful girl on his arm. I remember thinking how on earth did he pull a stunner like her? She seemed so out of place in this setting and was certainly over dressed for the normal clientele that frequented the pub.

Her husband was named Ross and didn't even give her the time of day! He was too wrapped up in playing darts and showing off his prowess to all who would take an interest. This left Annette and I talking for most of the night, we seemed to get on very well from our first meeting.

When Ross came over at the end of the night, it was as if a black cloud had come over Annette, her personality completely changed. At first she had been a witty, caring, interesting and confident woman, now she turned into a woman who seemed to shrink physically and emotionally into the shadows.

Over the next few weeks, the relationship with my parents had totally disintegrated, to the point where I needed my own space. Ross suggested that I spend some time at the flat, which he and Annette rented, but I would still have the freedom to go home whenever I wanted. This seemed like a good compromise, it certainly got me out of the frequent rows that Dad and I seemed to have on a regular basis.

When I moved into the flat, I realised that Ross and Annette were married in name only. Ross often went off with other women, only coming home when it suited him. They had a tiny baby, not many months old, but he spent more time with his girlfriends than he ever did with his wife and son.

Annette and I started going to the park or shopping. We soon realised that we were becoming the answer to each other's loneliness and insecurities. We allowed ourselves to get close and shared more and more time together.

After a while, we were able to confide in each other. Annette started to tell me of the beatings which she had received from Ross whenever he came home from one of his girl friends. She showed me her arms and legs, which were covered in bruises old and new.

I now understood the reason for the way she had reacted at the bar, the first time that I had met her. It was only a matter of time until the inevitable happened! We had fallen head over heels in love. We seemed to be the answer to each others longings. Despite my upbringing in old fashioned values, it wasn't long before we were inseparable.

About this time Ross went off on a long vacation with one of his girl friends. Annette moved back to her parents' home where we continued to go out with each other. The only difference was that we were able to have her parents as baby sitters. Since Ross had made the decision not to return, we had started to make plans about our future as a family.

We had spoken about an early engagement and what could happen after I had completed my initial training. Depending on where I was posted, we were looking forward to being together in married quarters and so we had made the most of our last few days together before I left.

Chapter 11

Mike Joins the Army

I was joining the army on a 6/22-engagement, meaning my assignment was in total twenty-two years. But I only had a commitment to six years in regular service; the rest would be on the reserve.

The branch of the army I was enlisted in was REME, Royal Electrical Mechanical Engineers and my trade training was as a Metalsmith, whatever that meant.

Because of my love of motorbikes I had originally expressed the wish to be a mechanic. However, there were no vacancies. I also found out later that there was a desperate shortage of Metalsmiths, due to the heavy work that was involved in it.

However, I found that it suited me and my temperament to a tee! Due to the fact that I was able to beat any frustrations I had out on to the anvil, with a sixteen pound sledge hammer, instead of the person who had upset me!

Arriving at Arborfield Garrison, which is close to Reading, I soon realized that there was no grace period for settling in. From the moment we arrived we knew – you're in the army now soldier! This became apparent when we were met by the duty Corporal who tried to quick march us from the guardhouse to our home for the next ten weeks!

What a shambles we were, left leg, left arm going together stumbling over each others feet, bumping into those at the side of us, what a mess! The Corporal wasn't in the least impressed.

The barracks were called Spiders due to the fact that they were built - if that's the right word - with a centre building and six similar legs off – three to the left and right sides, made totally of creosoted timber. Our names were called out and each of us allocated to one of the legs.

It's strange isn't it? The way that different people react when put into an unfamiliar situation. As each day passed, I had come to realize that I didn't need to look down at myself. The army was the great leveller; I was beginning to learn how to fit in with different temperaments, different attitudes, different beliefs and aspirations. At the same time, I was growing in self belief and respect for others. By the time I went home after ten weeks of training, I was unrecognizable as the person that had left home such a short time ago.

My parents and several of my family and friends attended the Passing Out Parade. When I marched across the square, with the rest of the squad, the thoughts of what we had achieved, since that first painful march to the barrack room until now, caused us all to swell with pride.

As I stepped forward as the first note was played, I knew that I had been prepared for whatever the future held, or was I?

Wait and see.

* * 🌀 * *

Going home on leave was quite an experience, with parties with my best friend Keith and my brother-in-law who was in the Air Force. All the normal jesting that happens when a soldier meets an airman. Things like "Brylcreeme boys" and "Muck wallower" were some of the more repeatable phrases that were used.

We caused havoc, by pretending we were at loggerheads and then laughing all the way home! But, under all of that, there was anticipation of going to my first posting at Bordon, in Hampshire.

The purpose of this was to complete initial trade training, which meant that for the next nine months

I would be living a very different way of life to basic training. There would be training on a firing range, a tough schedule of work projects, guard duties and fitness training.

So, I really appreciated the opportunity of going home to see Annette, who was always somewhere at the forefront of my thoughts. This generally happened about every two weeks, spending quality time with Annette and her young son. Soon, I hoped, they would be a permanent part of my life, if everything went as I planned.

Learning a trade for the first time was really rewarding and encouraging. I didn't waste any of the time I had and worked at every opportunity that was presented to me.

My favourite part of the training was blacksmithing. There was a real sense of achievement each time I took a piece of iron or steel and crafted something useful from it.

Soon we came to the end of the course and the exams. There were both practical and theory exams to overcome, thankfully I was successful in both.

So now came the exciting bit! – going out to a Unit to use all the various skills I had learned in the last nine months. We were given our postings after being told some of the different ones which were on offer. Places like attachments to commando or parachute regiments, which were soon snapped up by the gung-ho types.

Personally, I couldn't wait to use my trade skills and really didn't much mind where I went. Eventually I was given a posting, Detmold in North West Germany. I was given two weeks Embarkation Leave before reporting to my new unit.

On arrival in Germany, I soon realized that I liked the idea of travel, seeing new and exciting places and people. Detmold was a pretty German town, but the population were outnumbered by the large amount of troops who were billeted there.

What I hadn't bargained for, was how much free time I would have and what a heavy drinking environment it was that I had come into. Above every barrack block was a bar in which all idea of normal measures of spirit went out of the window. Every single shot was measured as a generous double and a double as an enormous four shots!

How easy I found it, to go along with this culture and return to my old drinking habits, but worse, I gradually went from liking drink, to needing drink. Drinking games became the norm and when the barrack bars weren't open, the bars down town were. So, sensible fun soon turned into a serious addiction.

As long as you were able to fulfil your duties, nothing was ever said. Senior Ranks were easy to fool, by making sure kit etc was prepared well in advance.

Christmas of 1972, I spent back in the United Kingdom. I had what can only be called a memorable celebration of my 21st birthday!

I tripped over my Sisters' long handled handbag while dancing and fell head first through a plate glass window. The party culminated in receiving twenty stitches in my back at the local hospital and much help, love and support from Annette.

I found out later, Annette had become pregnant. We had talked a lot about her joining me in Germany, so it seemed natural to start to put plans into place for our marriage. I went back to barracks in January very excited.

However, it was going to be a long wait because for the next three weeks I wasn't able to get in touch with Annette. When I did, it was to hear that she was not going to do any of the things we had spoken about. Instead, she had gone back to her ex-husband. (You will recall! the one that beat her black and blue!) She wouldn't say anything else, so I was left with no means of contact. Although I continued to write, I soon found out that I wasn't going to get a reply to those either, my world fell apart!

I turned once again to drink for solace but could find none; a week later I went into one of the barrack bars nicknamed "The Beasty Bar".

In this bar, there was an inauguration ritual, where you had to drink a boot full of every liquid off the back of the bar. Yes, everything! So, as any normal sensible male would do, I said I was up for the challenge. How stupid can we be and still have a brain? And all because of pride or ego.

Anyway, there I was, sitting on a barstool and was given this 'Nig drink' as it was called. So, facing the bar, I drank the full contents of the boot. I felt myself falling backwards but couldn't stop myself! I can't remember much else, but I was later told that I cracked my head on the steel rim of a beer barrel table, directly behind me and then crashed to the floor unconscious.

The next thing I remember was two days later, after waking up in a hospital bed, to hear a comment from one of the doctors who said "So, you are alive!" I felt awful, I ached, was sore and my throat didn't feel as though it belonged to me.

When I became fully conscious, the doctor said they had to use a stomach pump on me to remove the rubbish I had drunk, which I later found out included Brasso metal cleaning fluid and numerous other concoctions.

He also said that they had lost vital signs for a while. "You should be dead" he said.

From then on, I made a rapid recovery and was sent back to camp. Only to be met by the warrant officer, who told me to get into No 1 dress for Co's Orders. In army language the equivalent of being called in front of God. He has the power to expel, jail, fire or all three and more as he wishes.

I was marched in, and slammed to attention. I was expecting the worst and felt very stupid and sheepish. But the Co looked favourably at me, for two reasons, one, my impeccable service record and two, that I had already had enough punishment, both before and after, going into the hospital.

So, with a promise to go tee total, I was let off with a verbal warning. Well, I soon learned that I couldn't change something by just giving my word. The power that drink had over me was far greater!

Or to put it another way 'If you want to change some things in your life, you've got to change some things in your life "If you keep on doing what you've always done, you'll keep on getting what you've always got"

Chapter 12

A Brand New Start

One night I went to see Terry, a guy who had become my friend, confidant and drinking partner. I said to him "Are you coming down town"? He said, looking straight at me, "What do you want me to come with you for? All you want to do is get blasted out of your mind!"

That caught me off guard and for the first time I had to think about my reasons for my actions. I had not had to do that for a while. What I didn't know, was that this was the night that would change the way I lived my life forever.

My reply was that I needed someone I could trust, to help me get back home. Which, looking back, really sounds a pathetic excuse from a so called adult male, but nevertheless Terry agreed to come with me.

So, off we went on the normal pub crawl around the local German Inns. After drinking at three quarters of them, I realized that the alcohol was having no effect.

In fact, it seemed that everything that was going on in my life at that time, began to come into clear focus - much to my annoyance, after all, why would anyone go out drinking to get sober?

The last inn that we went into was called the Marienecke and was probably the favourite of all my locals. There was a good local clientele who were accommodating and friendly to us, the drink was always first class and the food excellent.

It was an icy cold February night and was just turning midnight. Inside there was a great big open fire with an ample supply of large logs, that thoroughly warmed the spacious lounge and bar area.

We ordered our drinks and sat down to talk as we had so often done before, little knowing what was to come next. Terry and I were chewing over what had been happening in my life, when suddenly, out of the blue, he says "Why don't you try God for the answer?"

"Don't be stupid!" I exclaimed, "He doesn't exist."

But in that instant, I began to realise that although I had said I didn't believe in Him, I also realised that if there was any chance that God existed, I certainly needed Him at this moment!

My mind went into overdrive, I started to talk in my head, "Lord if you're real, prove yourself to me, if you do, I'll commit my life to you" (The room as I have said, was hot!) I now know that what I did is called putting out a fleece, or putting down a challenge. What I said was, "Lord I want to feel cold, but not just me, Terry as well!"

It took only a matter of seconds until I started to feel a chilling cold; I felt as though I had been frozen, I had never felt so cold before!

(Remember the prayer was in my head between God and Me!) I turned to Terry and said, "I'm really feeling cold", to which he replied "So do I". So, I told Terry what had happened, and he said, "What do you want to do about it?" I said "Let's go to the Church". He said, "The Garrison Church stays open 24 hours, will that do?" I said "Yes." So off we went.

As we walked into the empty church, Terry asked if I wanted him to stay. I said "Yes, pray for me" So I went up to the altar and got down on my knees, I tried hard to speak but I just began to fill up inside.

Suddenly, all that had happened in the past hour or so started to make an impact. I came to the realization, that not only was God real but He must care for me to come and answer my prayer when I'm in the middle of trying to get totally drunk.

On top of that, my life hadn't especially been a flowery picture card. I also knew that if this God was as big as He appeared, I had made a bargain with Him and perhaps I shouldn't take lightly the promises I had made to Him a short while before.

As I reflected on these things, I was left speechless and the only thing I could do was to sob out I'm sorry. In front of me, something like a video began to run, showing all the lousy incidents in my life. As each scene appeared, I managed to sob out, "I'm sorry."

The tape just continued to run for what seemed a lifetime and as each filthy memory came to mind I felt more and more ashamed but still all I could find to say was, "Sorry."

Then the tape stopped, so I stood up and as I started to walk down the aisle to where Terry was still in prayer, I felt as though I was walking on air!

I felt clean, refreshed, and light, as though I had lost a heavy weight from my shoulders! Now, I wanted to sing and dance and shout, all at the same time, at 4am in the morning!! Totally sober, eyes that were clear, apart from the tears of joy that were running freely down my face! I knew I was free, at that moment!

WOW! WOW! What happened? I'd never felt like this ever!

I went to the room that I shared with three others and as I walked in, I was greeted by the gross pornography that covered the lockers in the room, as it did in most barrack rooms. For the first time, it offended my spirit, it felt wrong and for the first time, dirty. I tore it all down and threw it into the bin, likewise the library of books that stood on my bookshelf, which were equally seedy.

I was known at that time as 'The Librarian' and had always got a good supply of raunchy and gutter press types of novels, which, as I later looked back, realised were a total waste of time and money. Having completed the clear out of the things that felt wrong, I then went to bed and slept effortlessly for the first time, like a baby.

I woke up at 6 am, went to a full English breakfast, changed into uniform, and went on parade ready and on time and after the parade to the workshop, with no bottles of booze to put in cold water for the morning. I started to weld and as I looked through the glass on my mask, realized that this was the first time I was completely sober doing my job.

The date was **February 20th 1973** which was the beginning of Mike Deakin becoming the man that he was born to be! And they all lived happily ever after? Dah! That only happens in fairy stories and this isn't one of those!

From that time on, I came to know Jesus in the same way you would know a best friend. I got to know Him more and more as I literally devoured the bible. I read it like a hungry man searching for a something to eat, a thirsty man in a desert and the more I read, the more I wanted to read and the more I learned the more I wanted to be with Him.

I talked to Him about everything, even the tiny, seemingly insignificant things and in this way I found a new love of life and everything started to fall into place and became more balanced.

As time went on, the people I served with began to realize that something significant had happened in me. They started to ask me questions and I began to see that even the ones who tried to take the Mickey, or seemed to have it 'all together' wanted to know the answers as to why I was so happy all the while.

Mike Re-born!

To Have and To Hold

It was quite comical at times, because the guys who knew my past drink problem had avoided asking me to go out with them. One day I challenged them on their behaviour. They said, "But you don't drink anymore" I said, "Can't I drink coke or orange?" They said, "Won't you feel out of place?" I assured them that my not drinking was more of a problem to them, than it was to me. From that time I was invited to join them and was told that I was worse when sober, than they were when they were drunk! Jesus had given me life to the full!

I enjoyed every minute of this new life! Every day was a new adventure! I started to excel in my trade and every other area of army life. One day while discussing my lack of educational ability, one of the guys challenged me to go to the education block to make good the deficiencies.

So, I took the challenge, I started courses in English, Maths and German and achieved passes in all three! A.C.E. Army Certificate of Education, not bad, I thought, for a dropout who would never achieve anything?

It has always been one of the great privileges, to share the amazing testimony of the way my life has been turned around and encourage others to aim high.

I often say to people, "Don't let anyone set your sights lower than you believe, inside there lives a seed of greatness, yes! Even in you"!

I was aided in my new way of life by the constant friendship and fellowship of other Christians on camp, who encouraged me as a young Christian.

Chapter 13

Celia Arrives in Münster

I reached Münster and settled in and then phoned Simon to let him know what had happened. He, of course had already heard the garbled version through the grapevine, but I explained that I was using this opportunity to prove our true feelings for each other.

I settled in quite happily and found my way into the town. It was much more what I'd envisioned Germany to be like, although much of the town had been bombed during the war, it had been rebuilt to restore its original character.

Simon and I had booked a weeks' leave in February, to go home and make preparations for our Wedding in April. I was still unsure, but was swept up with it all, so I booked my flight and went home.

Simon joined me there, where we went visiting relatives. We went up to London, where I met up with my friend, Mal, who was to be my bridesmaid, and we went to a Bridal Hire shop, to look at the dress I had chosen,

I tried it on, liked it and paid the deposit. Then we went to look for bridesmaids dresses, we found some we liked and put down a deposit on those, too.

Simon and I went to a Show, and then caught the night train to Cornwall to visit his parents. We arrived early morning and walked through the little seaside town to their house. I don't remember very much more, except feeling very tired and his Mum offering me the chance to lie down for an hour. Sleep, however, eluded me, my emotions were in turmoil! I turned to my New Testament and Psalms; it was a Living Bible translation. I had been reading Psalms as my daily reading; today it was Psalm 16, where it reads,

"The Lord Himself is my inheritance, my prize. He is my food and drink, my highest joy! He guards all that is mine. He sees that I am given pleasant brooks and meadows as my share! What a wonderful inheritance! I will bless the Lord who counsels me; He gives me wisdom in the night. He tells me what to do. I am always thinking of the Lord; and because He is so near, I never need to stumble or fall. Heart body and soul are filled with joy. ... You have let me experience the joys of life and the exquisite pleasures of your own eternal presence".

I began to weep, as I realised that David, the Psalmist, had a far more wonderful relationship with God than I had ever dreamed was possible. I prayed and asked God to take control of my situation and to make things clear to me.

We returned home and a couple of days later, I was due to fly back to Germany, but due to an industrial dispute, the Airline I was due to fly with were grounded. So, I phoned QARANC HQ and let them know, and they said they would be in touch.

That gave us an extra day, or so. Simon decided that he would go into town to get my engagement ring valued, (he had bought it in Germany). I stayed home with Mum and whilst I was helping her put away the linen, I said, "You know, Mum, I'm not sure if I'm doing the right thing". She replied, "You don't have to go through with it, you know, if you're not happy." Suddenly, it was like someone had flicked a power switch!

I turned to her and I said, "No, I don't do I? That's it! Finished! It's over!" I was flooded with relief; I knew at last that I had made the right decision.

The date? 20th February 1973, could it just be coincidence that in Detmold, a young man had just given his life to the Lord? It was the first of what we called, "God-incidences"!! Another key had been turned in Heaven!

A couple of days later, I was able to fly back to Germany and arrived in Münster with a spring in my step and a song in my heart!

Mike and Celia Deakin

Meanwhile, my Mum and Dad were offered a Parish in Norfolk, where they had visited on holiday. They accepted and moved into a large, chilly old Rectory, in a village near Norwich.

My leave was still booked for April, so I decided that it was an ideal time to visit Amsterdam! Münster was an easy train journey away, so I jumped on the train with the intention of finding cheap accommodation on arrival. However, I hadn't realised just how popular a destination it was in the Spring.

I got chatting to an elderly Dutch lady, who was seeing off her sister at the Station. To my surprise, she invited me to stay with her, as the accommodation bureau could only offer a place in Den Helda, in the north of Holland, which she assured me, was miles away!

I stayed for about four days and took in all the sights, then caught a flight to Norwich. This became a favourite way of getting home, as it gave me 5 or 6 hours in Amsterdam before I needed to get the train back to Münster.

I also booked to attend a SASRA Whitsun Conference, in June, at Church House, RAF Wegburg.

The Search for Happiness

In the past I had often cried,
It seemed that love from me could hide.
I searched the world for one to care
For someone who my life would share.
But long ago and far away,
There in a manger filled with hay
*Lay the one who now fills my life_*
Drove from my soul all fear and strife.

For Jesus died on Calvary
So now I am from sin set free!
He rose! The Victor, from the grave!
All who come to Him, He will save.

When first I gave my life to Him
And pandered not to every whim
Into my heart He came to live,
Love and peace to my soul He gives.
Could it be so? I could not see.
The Lord Himself was love to me.
Yet still I sought for human love
In Men, despising God above

But I found that sinful action,
Could not bring me satisfaction.
My Lord required sacrifice
"Seek ye first the Kingdom of Christ".
Now, no more to dances I went
But much more time in prayer I spent.
Seeking after His righteousness
I found eternal happiness!

Blessed was I, with a love untold!
Kept safe by Him within the fold.
*With other folk who love the Lord_*
Bound me to Him with Silver Cord.

Caused another to seek His face
Now see it written, "Saved by Grace!"
Drew him, too, and gently bound him
To the Holy One Who found him.
The Lord knows what the future holds
As us together, now He moulds.
Man and wife, to be together
With God's blessing, now, forever!

Written by Celia in Münster 1973

Chapter 14

Boy Meets Girl

The morning meeting had been good and after lunch I made my way down to the coffee bar, I didn't know anyone there at the time, but there were a few folk sitting at the bar drinking coffee. I sat on my own watching them, thinking. I had come to the Whitsun Conference looking for some answers, some direction for my life. There had been a box placed for questions, so they could be addressed during the Weekend.

So, I had put in my question as follows:-

Q. Should I keep praying for a husband, or should I just accept that God wants me to stay single?

Well, by a process of elimination, the leaders had worked out who had put in the question, and tactfully taken me aside. Not an encouraging sign, I thought, as I was now 25 years old and feeling like I was "on the Shelf"! But the answer they gave me was actually quite encouraging! I was asked, "Has God specifically told you that you are to stay single? No? Then the "Norm" is that most people get married, so, yes, keep praying. It may be closer than you think!"

Suddenly, I was aware of the conversation at the bar. They were talking about an alternative tune to an old Hymn. A tall, slim young man with dark curly hair, was talking avidly, "Yes", he said, "There's a tune to 'When I survey, the wondrous cross, on which the Prince of Glory died. It goes like this…"and he began to sing, the others didn't know the tune, but I did, so moving towards the bar, I joined in. We sang in perfect harmony to the end of the song.

After a little ripple of applause, someone said, "Voices blend, so do lives." We introduced ourselves, he was Mick and I was Celia, and we chatted with the others for a while, before the evening meal. Later, when I went into the meeting, Mick had saved a seat for me. So, we spent time together, and co-wrote new, Christian words for the "Theme from Love Story", which we sometimes sing together.

For me, although he seemed like a bit of a rough diamond, I recognised that although he had only been a Christian just over 3 months, he was growing fast, and had the kind of leadership skills that I could follow.

All too soon, it was time to leave, but we exchanged addresses. I went back to Münster, not really expecting to hear from him again.

About a week later, I received a letter from him. Now, I was never the worlds' greatest letter writer, but it just so happened that I was on Night Duty, on the Psychiatric Unit, where my role was that of Chaperone, as it was a mixed unit. This meant that I had loads of time on my hands, so although I meant to write a short note, it actually ended up as a five page letter, telling him my life story!

A few letters later, I invited him to Münster, having arranged for him to stay on camp with the Medics. So, on the Friday evening, I went to the Station to meet the train, but he wasn't on it! I didn't know what to do, it wasn't a good place to hang around and I didn't know if he had maybe changed his mind.

I did like all girls do when they've been "stood up"; I went home and washed my hair! So when one of my friends came to tell me there was a fellow at the door asking for me, I had wet hair, wrapped in a towel! That's how I went down to greet him!! He wasn't at all put off, but handed me a bunch of flowers!

I sat him in the sitting room, while I got myself ready. I don't remember what we did that evening, probably we went to the NAAFI but on the Saturday, we went to Münster Zoo, and on Sunday, we went over to see the Army Scripture Reader.

Mike and Celia Deakin

On the way, we talked about marriage and I laughingly told him that I already had a dress and a ring! It was true! Rather than loose my deposit for the dress, I had told the shop I was postponing the wedding….I didn't say I had to find another man first!!

Chapter 15

A Time for Commitment

Later on, Mick wrote again, telling me he was going to Spree 73 (**Sp**iritual **Re**-emphasis) a special event being run at Earls Court in London, by the Billy Graham Organisation; was I interested in going? I had some leave booked for the week following Spree, to go to Filey, but managed to arrange a week of Night duty, so I could go to London.

I wrote to some friends, to arrange to stay with them. I finished Nights on Monday morning, picked up my bags and headed for the airport. I arrived at their house in a downpour, to find no-one at home. Kind Indian neighbours took me in to await their return. I had not realised that it was August Bank Holiday; therefore my letter had not yet reached them.

I didn't have long to wait for their return and after a little confusion and excited greetings, I was finally able to grab a bite to eat and get my head down! I slept the clock round, finally surfacing at around 11 am Tuesday morning. So, I made plans to go to Earls Court, and got there in time for the evening concert but wasn't able to find Mick. I decided to just enjoy the concert, and trust that things would be resolved in the morning.

We had arranged to meet at the Spree 73 Conference at Earls Court. So, I arrived in London and on Bank Holiday Monday, went to register and got involved in a very full program of seminars and concerts.

I already had a seat booked, but since at that time we didn't live with a mobile phone glued to our ear, I had no way of knowing where Celia was or when she would be arriving. The seat number proved irrelevant because of the format of the conference, so she had no way of finding me. So, we both separately did what any normal Christian would do, we said, "God, if it's your will, you sort it out".

On Tuesday, knowing which seminars I had been allocated to, I went in and got involved in all the various activities which were going on. Wednesday morning whilst sitting in the seminar, Celia arrived and registered and was allocated to the same seminar as me though she didn't know that! She followed the signs through the building and walked straight in ending up sitting in the empty seat beside me, without either us knowing how!

We spent the whole of the next few days going out doing different evangelistic projects and started to find out more about each other. It soon became obvious that we both had a real heart for evangelism and seemed to be able to work well together.

This was a really exciting time for both of us, as we saw the unfolding of the sovereign will of God working out, in and around us each day.

On the last evening, Billy Graham asked us all if we were ready to make a commitment to go anywhere, anytime to do anything for Him. I knew I wanted to do that, but would Mick? It was the acid test of our future relationship, to my relief after a minute or so, he stood beside me. Later, as he got on his motorbike, he said to me, "That was really scary! I don't know the what, where, or when, but whatever it is, I know we'll be doing it together."

After a Concert at Wembley Stadium, with Johnny Cash, at the end of the conference; we each set off to go and meet Celia's mom and dad, which had been previously arranged, prior to my coming over from Germany. Celia travelled by train. I rode my motorbike, my pride and joy, a BSA 250cc which I had ridden for countless miles.

During the journey I had plenty of time to review the things that had happened at the conference and started to consider the meeting with mom and dad. I decided that I needed to concentrate on the road ahead and let the rest take its own path, which of course, I believed was being guided by our great and mighty God.

This break turned out to be a real time of bonding together, getting to know each others little foibles. After a further few days at Celia's parents house we decided we were ready to get engaged (this could have been influenced by the fact that her mother said she felt that Celia would end up left on the shelf), private joke.

This was also the point where Mick became Mike, as I said I wasn't one of his workmates!

Celia decided she had done enough army and that she would take the option to leave before we got married in July 1974.

During our engagement, we often travelled to Bielefeld to stay with our friends, John and Pam in order to see each other and we were looking forward to settling down in Germany. However, the Army had other ideas; I was given a posting to Tidworth at the end of April.

To Have and To Hold

Celia's father was a minister in the Church of England and since he wanted to give her away wasn't able to take the wedding service as well. There were a few jokes about swapping hats, "Who giveth this Woman?" Swap hats, "I do"! But instead, we asked a family friend to take the service for us! The ceremony was taken at her dads church, which was a typical stained glass decorated, wooden pewed country parish Church.

Celia & Mike with Celia's Mum & Dad

What a way to set out into the most influential relationships on earth, to have and to hold, to love with all my heart, soul and possessions till death do us part, union for life, for richer or poorer, well, like most of us that get married, as far as I was concerned, I had meant every word spoken.

How many of us have had the chance of tuition on life? Most of the instruction of how to be a parent or a partner in life, as indeed in any other relationship comes from watching our parents and a lot of trial and error! Yet we so often make promises to each other without really sitting down to assess the timing or the truth of the words we speak?

After getting married we enjoyed a honeymoon spent on the picturesque coastline of East Anglia, a little place called Mundsley, just down from Cromer. While we were there, the Lord gave us some promises from Isaiah Ch 43, which have often been given to us since.

"Fear not, for I have redeemed you; I have called you by your name; you are mine.

When you pass through the waters I will be with you; and through the rivers, they shall not overflow you. When you walk through the fire, you shall not be burned, nor shall the flame scorch you.'

'You are my witnesses', Says the Lord, 'And my servant whom I have chosen.'

'Remember not the former things, nor consider the things of old. Behold, I will do a NEW THING, now it shall spring forth. Shall you not know it?'"

What a blessing that God didn't reveal the full significance of those words until much later.

Aren't you glad that you don't know the future? We just have faith in the One Who holds the future, and leave it up to Him to show us when the time is right.

They were also repeated to us on the first morning Mike went back to work. "' Behold, I will do a new thing.'" So, we said that God must be underlining it with His red pen!

Chapter 16

We've Only Just Begun...

I set out for Tidworth on the motorbike and Celia followed on by train to Andover. Tidworth is a typical forces town with all the normal necessities including shops, banks and of course the lifesaver in so many camps, the NAAFI, the get anything store. It is situated on the Salisbury plain, which over the next couple of years we really came to love.

When I arrived in Tidworth, I had gone to the camp to sort myself out, only to be told that my unit was just about to leave for Cyprus on emergency attachment. So, if I didn't want to leave my bride for an unspecified time, I should make myself scarce until the advance party had gone. I was still on leave until then anyway, so that's what I did.

Due to the circumstances, we weren't able to get army accommodation immediately, anyway. However, my sergeant, Mick, offered me the chance for us to stay at his house.

To Have and To Hold

He was, by then, on his way to Cyprus so his wife, Margaret and Celia managed to get along reasonably well, while I was enjoying myself at work ha-ha!

When I arrived back at camp, after finishing my leave, I was placed on the rear party. All we seemed to do day after day for the duration was clean, polish, or paint green, grey or black, how exciting is that?

The tour of Cyprus only lasted about eight weeks but in that time we had secured lodgings in a very quaint picturesque part of the country called Shrewton, which was in the vicinity of Stonehenge.

This all came about through another one of those coincidences, you know, the ones I didn't believe in. The story goes like this, about three weeks into the Cyprus tour we went to visit a pen pal of Celia's, who was working on a stud farm, caring for the horses.

The day we went to see Evelyn, the pen pal, coincided with the SASRA day of prayer. They had said that they would pray for a place for us to live. When we arrived, Evelyn was not at home, but we met the owner of the property who kindly looked after us.

Completely out of the blue she said you're not looking for a place to live, are you? As any normal person would say to a stranger who turns up unannounced, to see a student of yours!

Of course, I understand its just coincidence, oh yeah! We were given a guided tour of two bedrooms, a lounge, and kitchen. It was small but adequate for our needs. The beautiful outlook into the surrounding countryside was just an excellent bonus to all the above.

We snapped her hand off at being offered this chance of such surroundings, it's worthy to note, that at this time we had nothing towards making a home, all our belongings were still on their way from Germany.

So, as many young couples, we started married life with borrowed cutlery, two plates, two cups and saucers, and a cookery book! Incidentally everything is provided in married quarters, which is what we were expecting when we arrived in Tidworth.

On the way back to camp we went to the house of the Scripture Reader. After explaining the day's events, all present were surprised, amazed and happy at the quick answer to their prayers! We moved in the following week!

During our time at Shrewton, we had a visit from David, a friend from the camp. We later discovered that David always managed to turn up just as we were about to sit down for a meal, it became a standing joke. You know the sort of thing I'm sure you can smell the cooking, etc!

To Have and To Hold

Well, on this occasion he came to welcome us into the house and we said, "You could have eaten with us but we have no extra cutlery," at which he said, "Just a minute" and disappeared outside. He came back with knife, fork and spoon!

(His story!) As he was leaving barracks, he stopped at his motorbike, turned off the engine, went back to his room and picked up his cutlery not knowing why, well, you judge, coincidence?

After a few weeks we left our idyllic hideaway to go into proper married quarters at Tidworth camp. We soon settled in and started to make friends both in work and the neighbourhood.

We especially clicked with a Christian Officer and his wife, Don and Anne, who told us "We are Pentecostal/Anglicans!! Which kind of sums them up, slightly zany, but quite sedate. "Excuse me, but Hallelujah!!" was a phrase they often used!

They both had this easy grace of being able to get along with anyone, no matter what their rank or station in life. Their house was always filled with young Christians in the evenings or weekends, or young Mums on a Wednesday morning. They welcomed us and we felt very much at home with them.

We also joined a House Church, which met in Durrington. When Mike had mentioned to me about being in a group where the Holy Spirit was moving, with prophecies and speaking in tongues, I felt uneasy. But when I opened my bible that first morning, to find the words "Behold I will do a new thing" Isaiah Ch 43 v19, I felt that God was assuring me, that it was all in His hands.

We went to visit Pete and Gwen, whose home the house church was hosted by, and I was greeted by the most lovely couple. Peter was like a great cuddly teddy bear, with a wonderful musical gift on the piano and a ridiculous sense of humour!

Whilst Gwen was a quiet but strong personality who gently but firmly guided us into the ways of God. Really, for the first time, here was someone who didn't just teach us the bible, but one who truly *discipled* us; *"Wrestling in prayer till Christ be formed in us". Galatians Ch 4: v19 (My paraphrase)* As a result we began to grow in Grace.

I decided that I should be Baptised, something I had always resisted, saying that I had been Christened and Confirmed; so I believed I had verified the promises made on my behalf as an infant. However, God had said to me, "If this was the only thing I wanted you to do for me, would you be willing?" So, I said yes, and was Baptised in the river Avon, much to the disapproval of my parents.

About a month after my Baptism, Mike had to go away on manoeuvres for about 5-6 weeks. During that time I read a book called 'From Prison to Praise', by Merlin Currothers. I read about how God can change situations when we praise Him despite the situation, instead of moaning or pleading. Then he explained about the Baptism in the Holy Spirit, I prayed the prayer in the book, and then opened my mouth, like he said, and began to make sounds. Well, I felt stupid, decided that it was all from my mind and I disbelieved. I never thought any more about it until a year later when Mike and I were in Devon.

One of the favourite things that we did as a couple was to entertain. Sundays, we always had a full house and in army circles, the single guys and girls don't need much persuasion, to come and eat you out of house and home, play board games and just talk.

The varied interesting conversations about lifestyle and background, never ceased to enthral us, we became like the family that they had never known or simply, were missing.

Work went well and I made progress in every area of army life, I enjoyed sport, badminton, table tennis, etc. I should say at this stage that my temperament was that of someone always moving, my favourite phrase became Let's go! It didn't matter where, just "Lets go". It probably showed that I needed to achieve, move forward all the time. As I look back, I can see that I probably wasn't the easiest character for Celia to deal with, as she is very much more laid back and home loving.

I spent a lot of time away on army manoeuvres and in 1975 had a six-month tour in Belfast Northern Ireland. This tour was hard work, but I loved the challenge. Working anything between ten to sixteen hours a day was quite normal, so I guess I didn't spend much time sleeping! I have always thrived on hard work and long hours.

In September, I managed to get rest and recuperation leave, so, I flew home and Celia had booked a caravan for a week. So, off we went to Devon, in our 3 wheeler Reliant... via London? To take a family friend back home?!!

Chapter 17

Just like being Born Again!

For a short time we, were free to enjoy the simple things. For me, that meant not having to carry a weapon every time I went out and not having to watch my back, if I came into an unfamiliar group of people.

While we were in Devon we went into the countryside, and sat on a sunny hillside. Celia was talking to me about all that had been going on at home, when she suddenly became aware that there were no answers coming from me.

There we were, in the middle of nowhere, surrounded by God's glorious creation, and in the middle of the conversation, all of the last four months caught up. I went out like a light! I was unconscious of everything, including poor Celia.

On the Sunday, we met some Christians who were holding an impromptu Open Air Service on the beach at Exmouth. They invited us to join them at the Conference being held at their hotel, which we did. There was a man preaching called Cecil Cousins, who was part of Fountain Trust.

We went along to a couple of the meetings, just glad to have some fellowship and sound teaching. He quoted a scripture which I had often heard before but had never thought it applied to me, "All your righteousnesses are as filthy rags." And I suddenly realised that all my self effort to be good enough for God were just that...filthy rags. I repented, saying "I'm sorry for the way I've lived, I don't want to be like that any more, I've tried my best, but now I see that even my best can never be good enough."

Everything Cecil had said, had witnessed with my spirit that it was true but there was just this question about the Baptism in the Holy Spirit, which I wasn't sure about. Mike, having spoken to Cecil and a lady called Iris, was satisfied that it was right and that he wanted them to pray for him to receive The Holy Spirit.

I still wasn't sure, so Mike found Iris after the meeting, and explained the situation. They found me at the bookstall, and I found myself telling her about reading "From Prison to Praise" and my prayer and failed attempt to speak in tongues, finishing lamely, "...and I disbelieved". Having thus confessed my unbelief, Iris suggested, that she just pray for me to have peace about it all.

Well, I got peace all right, bucket loads!! As she started to pray for me, I felt this joy welling up in my stomach, it just bubbled up and up until it came out of my mouth like a spring of living water, a whole new, unlearned language!

At this, Mike became very excited, and so we turned to pray for him, but he could not receive at that time. Iris sent us home with instructions to Mike to "Ask Celia to pray for you to receive." This was something of a blow to his masculine pride, but after a while, and getting right before the Lord, he asked me to pray. I did so, and Mike began to speak in tongues. He kept waking in the night and pinching himself to see if he could still do it!

He was up with the lark, and jumped into the car to go to the hotel, where he bounced in on them at breakfast, saying, "I've got it! I've got it!"

All too soon, our time had gone, but as we drove home, I didn't have that dread of the Parting and the separation that I had before when he went. Then I was in tears every time I thought about him leaving, but I knew things were different now. We were different!

We called in to Pete and Gwen's and Gwen knew something had happened as we walked in. We sat down and explained what had happened. I followed Gwen into the kitchen. "It was just like being born again!" I told her. "Yes, Dear," she said, "That's right."

It was about a week later, I was thinking about what Gwen had taught us, "The Spiritual always follows the natural," that I realised, "Well, there's life before birth, isn't there? So, I *was* born again, Wow!!!"

Mike had returned to duty in Northern Ireland for two more months. Once he was back in the workshop, it was back to not knowing what the next day or even the next minute could bring, literally anything could happen. But I knew that God was with him and with me and we just had to trust Him.

On my return home, after the 6 month tour, we started to go out to explore the surroundings, we could usually be found out with the House Church Group, walking over the hilltops of Salisbury Plain.

We were also often to be found down in Fordingbridge, with a family of three generations. These very dear friends, Bernard and Hazel were furniture restorers and a more loving, hospitable, caring family I have rarely, if ever, come across.

Many are the times when we have just turned up with another 'someone else' from camp, wanting to show them what being a Christian is really about, from a practical point of view.

To Have and To Hold

Hazel always rose to the occasion, putting a meal on the table for us all. Though we were often pressed into service to shell peas, or top'n'tail gooseberries! We also enjoyed listening to some really old records of country yokel comedy, which had us splitting our sides, and a good sing song around the piano, singing all the old Moody and Sankey hymns! This dear couple prayed for us every day, from that time and probably still do!

The following year, Mike had to go to Bordon on a Trade Training Course for 6 months. At least he was able to get home every other weekend. He finished the course in December and then we heard that his unit in Tidworth were being Posted to…..Bordon, in the Spring.

By the time a quarter came available, in April, I was 5 months pregnant. I packed all our belongings into large plywood crates, known as MFO Boxes, Mike hired a van, and he and a friend filled it, drove to Bordon, dumped the boxes and came back for the rest, plus me and the cat!

Mike was on the rear party, which meant he had to go back to Tidworth, and with some urgency, as the van had to be back by evening! So, you've guessed it! I was deposited at the flat along with the cat, huge boxes in all directions (one filled the kitchen) and, with my swelling tum, I wasn't as slim as I was!

I managed to set up a single bed and put some bedding on it, this took some time, so I went to bed and slept. The

Mike and Celia Deakin

problem of sorting it all out would just have to wait till morning.

I was just struggling to reach the sink, to make my morning cuppa, when the doorbell went. I went downstairs and opened the door to find Anne and one of the Christian girls on the doorstep.

"Good Morning, Mrs Deakin," said Anne, rolling her sleeves up,

"We've come to work! Is that all right?" I was just overwhelmed,

"You are the answer to the prayers of a Damsel in Distress!" I told them as we hugged on the doorstep,

"Come on in! You'll never know just how glad I am to see you!" They sorted everything out for me, shifted furniture, set up the bed, laid a carpet square down, arranged the lounge, and generally made it look like home!

It was about 3 or 4 weeks before Mike was able to join me and start working in Bordon. We joined a local Pentecostal church and were taken into the loving care and hospitality of the Pastor and his wife, Reg and Nancy.

We also occasionally went along to a large House Church Group who met in Reading. Don and Anne had moved to Farnborough in Hampshire, so they were not too far away so we were still able to see them sometimes.

To Have and To Hold

In August 1977 we had the great joy of the birth of our first child Philip. I was working at the training school in Bordon, which at least meant that I had five weeks summer holiday, to be with Celia and my new son! But as so often happens in the army, in November 1977, I was sent on a five-month tour in Londonderry, Northern Ireland, during probably one of the most important times for us. But nothing changes the onward march of the army.

By the time Mike returned from Derry, it was the end of March, and Philip was 7 months old, and didn't know his daddy.

Chapter 18

Back to Germany

In May 1978 we were on the move again, back to Germany. Well, at least I was on the move; Celia had a miscarriage and had to stay with her parents in Norfolk, until I had sorted out the quarters in July. Then Celia moved with Philip to become really for the first time, the family Deakin.

This was a really good time! We all grew to love Germany and many of the German people. We loved the atmosphere, the culture, life style and especially the food! Oh! The thought of those fantastic Kuchen (German cakes to the uninitiated). They really are superb, but I digress, I could digress all day with the thoughts of those amazing cakes.

We spent lots of time discovering some of the beauty of this great country and people. We were stationed in Werl, not far from Iserlohn and Dortmund. It was about 7 miles from the Möhne See, of Dam Busters fame, in a very pretty area.

To Have and To Hold

In September, we brought Mike's parents over, for a holiday. We wanted to give them an opportunity to see that there was a lot more to life, than the tiny capsule they had lived in until now.

They often referred to the holiday as significant and always said what a real treat it had been! Apart from Dad's service in Italy, during the War, it was the only time they went abroad in their lives.

We were able to take them to the new All Weather Zoo in Münster and show them a little slice of German life. It seemed that as we travelled around, they became more and more animated by what they were seeing. This was the one and only time we had the chance to share our life with them.

* * 🐾 * *

In the October of 1978 I had gone on manoeuvres in Northwest Germany. This was the beginning of the worst winter in twenty years! The temperature was minus 20 degrees, and the combined European forces decided to send us on our "jolly's" (holidays)!

They wanted us to dig holes which were 6' x 4' x 2' in frozen ground, so that we could play war games. Our sleeping quarters were the same holes mentioned above!

(Sheer luxury)! Anyway, we had our fun and were on our way home after about ten days holiday ha-ha!

So that we didn't clog up the transport system with our convoys, we would normally travel through the night or early morning. So, there I was at 05.30hrs, travelling along an empty Autobahn.

I was positioned as tail end Charlie, at 50kph, (about 35mph) driving a Landrover with trailer. I have all the equipment needed for my occupation, which included bottled oxygen, acetylene, a portable, petrol fed welder, four jerry cans of fuel, all my tools, not to mention equipment for survival.

Mike the Para, my co-driver, was sitting drinking tea from one of our flasks and all was well in our lives. Having been a motorcyclist, I am always aware of what's going on in my mirror, so I saw the enormous truck coming up behind us at quite a speed.

Suddenly, I could feel the Landrover gathering speed without me doing anything! The next thing I know, I have been thrown into the passenger seat, but I am now laying on the door, which is underneath me, everything is whirling with the sounds of scraping and braking!

Finally, I came to a standstill and climbed out of the door, which was above my head.

I then realized that Mike was not in the vehicle. I started to look in the direction that I had come from and started running to find him. He came running towards me shouting to find out if I was ok; we both were, except that I had blood from the back of my head.

It was then that I recalled that I had seen that the ignition was still switched on and that there was fuel running onto the road. I turned around and sprinted back to the Landover and switched off the key.

Mike called me away, so I went back towards him, at which there were several explosions and it seemed as though the whole Autobahn was on fire!! Mike explained to me fully what a xxxxxxxxxxxxxxxx fool I was; I could have been blown sky high!

It was only later, that I heard the full story. When the "Woofer", as they are known, (a lorry towing a trailer the same size), had hit the rear of my trailer, it had taken off the top and carried it on his bumper down the road for the next 100yds.

The wheels of the trailer had been pushed underneath the land rover, turning it onto its side and causing it to continue to travel on for another good many yards. In the impact, the oxygen bottleneck had broken off and shot the bottle down the road like a torpedo, the acetylene and fuel had ignited and blown the Land rover and trailer to smithereens!!

Mike and Celia Deakin

We then waited for a further six hours, still in shock, for recovery of our vehicle. The police, recovery driver, accident assessors all said you should both be dead!

Mike had no injuries, Me? Would you believe, a half-inch cut on the back on my head! How many coincidences were there involved in this accident? Too many to relate!

I just thank the Lord who holds me safe in His hands.

During the autumn of 1978, I also had to contend with a very trying event that was blown out of all proportion by the unit I was serving with.

It all started at a Pay Parade sometime in late September, when I found that there was a query about an amount of 20DM missing from my pay. I asked the Pay Clerk what it was, "Oh that's all right, it's to buy raffle tickets for the Corporals Mess Draw,"

"What draw?" I said "Who authorized withdrawal from my pay?"

"It's orders, direct from the RSM!" (often referred to by soldiers as God, what he says is Law).

"Don't worry about it, its only going to be for five months and all NCOs have got to pay it".

"Well this is one NCO that's not! So, please arrange for the funds to go back into my pay!"

"Now look Mike," he said, "don't kick up a fuss or your stripe's on the line!"

"If that's all my stripe is worth, then they can have it back," I replied,

"You'll have to go in front of the RSM." He said, "Arrange it!" I retorted! (Under no circumstances would anyone willingly put themselves on RSM orders!)

Well, with my best dress uniform, I marched in, not a clever action to take, so here goes, Laddie! The dreaded RSMs parade! He wanted to know what all this was about and gave me the opportunity to explain myself and to my great surprise allowed me to sit down to do this.

I answered as follows, "When I came into the army I had no real faith, but I was asked to swear on the bible. I wasn't sure I believed in a God I didn't know or that I would serve God, Queen and Country in that order."

"Whilst in the army, I have come to have faith in that same God. I believe the Bible I swore on and therefore adhere in my life to the things I read and believe. Gambling, in that case, I believe is wrong. Therefore, the raffle as a game of chance is not right for me." His reply was that he could see my point of view, but since the order to purchase tickets came from the Co of the unit, he would need to be the one to decide on the next step. This continued back and forth until

November 1978, when I was summoned to attend Co's orders with the possibility of losing rank.

As soon as I heard this, I spoke to the Chaplain, Peter, to ask his advice and related what had happened so far. His reply was that he would stand Co's orders with me, because if they took my stripe, he could no longer wear his pips, due to his total agreement with the stance I was taking.

Co's orders were really a repeat of the RSM's, with the conclusion that they didn't know what to do with me! This continued to hang in the balance through November, December and into January.

During this time, it was becoming obvious that there were people at all ranks that now saw that I wasn't trying to be clever, but rather standing for a principle. Often these fellow soldiers and officers would come into my workshop, to ask me about my faith, what an opportunity this was, to share with people who were my superiors! As an evangelist, I was very aware of the immense privilege that I had been afforded, to speak to people of these ranks and in this depth.

At the end of January or beginning of February, I was called by my warrant officer for best dress parade in front of CREME, the Colonel of the whole of REME, which was my Corp.

To Have and To Hold

So, I got dressed in best blues and bulled boots to attend orders! Most soldiers only wear best blues once or twice in their career. The Queens Parade and your funeral! This was the third time I had worn mine in less than six months, each time in front of higher rank, maybe the next stop was the Queen herself?

As I wheeled in to face CREME, I slammed to attention, He said "Stand easy." and offered me a seat, he said, "Corporal Deakin, we need to sort out this slight discomfort that you seem to have with this unit, don't you agree?"

"Yes Sir."

"Now, we have some good news and some bad news, what do you want to hear first?" "The bad news, Sir,"

"You're going to have to leave this Regiment, but we've found somewhere that, knowing the whole story, would welcome you, how do you feel about that?" "When, Sir?"

"Immediately, would that be a problem for you and your family?"

'No Sir.'

"Would you like to know the good news?"

'Yes please Sir,'

With this, he pushed an official document to me; I could hardly believe my eyes! It was my promotion to

Mike and Celia Deakin

full corporal, which meant a significant rise in my pay scale and overseas allowance!

"Just one more requirement, Deakin, you have to go to the draw this evening at the Cpls Mess. You need to go to the tailor first, to get your new jersey, which of course will show your new Rank, do you think you can do that Corporal Deakin?" "Yes sir!"

"Congratulations! And enjoy your evening!"

As you read on into this book, I invite you to see an unseen hand, moulding, making and shaping our lives! With no compunction, I give all the credit and praise to my only Lord, Jesus Christ.

Chapter 19

The Move to Düsseldorf

So, a week later, in February 1979, we moved as a family to work with an RCT regiment, (Royal Corps of Transport). The base was at a place called Duisburg, a city, very much in the industrial Rhineland.

However, our married quarter was just outside Düsseldorf, which sat like a queen on the beautiful Rhine. This posting, was one that all of us settled into very quickly, we loved the magnificence of the scenery, which was close to hand.

Düsseldorf, we described as a country city, with all the charm of an old town in the atmosphere and architecture, but all the facilities of a large thriving city. The river Rhine is enormous and I have many happy memories of just sitting or walking along and enjoying the activity of the river.

We found Christian brothers and sisters at a former cinema in Düsseldorf, known as Jesus Haus! The congregation was mainly German, but we discovered quite a lot of Americans there, who were singers with the local German Opera House.

We were invited to join them on Sunday evenings, at a beautiful Apartment, overlooking the Rhine. We were delighted by the old Gas lights and beautiful buildings along the tree lined avenues in that part of town.

The Apartment belonged to the most lovely lady you could hope to meet! Her name was Mary Lou, and we enjoyed many an evening there, though there was sometimes quite a discussion about which key the chorus should be sung in! With so many professional singers, they occasionally needed someone (like Mike) to just start singing! After the meeting, Mary Lou would serve Apfel Kuchen, in her beautiful dining room.

We thought she had everything, but she had a son who was damaged at birth, who could do nothing for himself. He was by then a young man of perhaps 18, and although she had enough money to pay for the best nursing care, she chose to nurse him herself. An unsung hero, she never complained, or allowed bitterness to poison her life. No, her life distilled sweetness in every drop.

As we left Mary Lou's apartment, carrying Philip, asleep in his sleeping bag, to walk to the car, we thanked God for her devotion both to her son and to her Lord Jesus.

To Have and To Hold

I would often go into town shopping, with Philip in his pushchair. I caught the bus at the end of our road, to town, where I would meet up with a German girl and her little boy. She had a CV2 Dianne "Duck" car, and she took us to a ladies fellowship group. Afterwards, when she dropped us off in town, we would mooch round the beautiful shops.

All the German ladies were very taken with Philip, and would cluck around him like broody hens! In the shops, they all seemed to have a stock of sweeties for" der kinde" which was lovely! They really seemed to love and welcome children! Philip was now beginning to talk, and would say "Guten Tag!" (Good day) and a few other little German phrases, which absolutely delighted them!

This whole tour was one that we thoroughly enjoyed in every way, but it was also a time for decision, because I found it more and more difficult to justify my continuing in the army and preaching a gospel of peace and love. So, with mixed feelings I put in my six-month notice to leave. Of course, as soon as you know that you've made a decision, you can't wait for the time to come.

The decision we had made was that we would follow our hearts to Nottingham and join the house church with a Christian couple we had met while in Germany.

Keith and Cynthia, had a little boy called Andrew, so it was good for Philip our son as well. There was quite a lot to arrange with shipping and pre-release courses.

Chapter 20

A New Life in Nottingham

By the time we left Germany, the owner of Metalwork Company, had already accepted me in principle. It was close to where Keith and Cynthia lived and the only requirement was, for a specialization welding upgrade, to cope with the mainly stainless steel and aluminium welding that this company were doing.

So everything was set up for return to civilian life. Over the next few years, I was going to find out that you can take the man out of the army, but it takes a long time to take the army out of the man! Don't get me wrong, I had gained many good things from my time in the army, but there were some things that I had gained which in civilian life, were not so good.

We stayed at first with John and Anne and their family. John is a Doctor in General Practice and was also the elder of the House Fellowship which we were to attend. This suited us in getting acclimatized to this new way of life, but it wasn't long before we were able

Mike and Celia Deakin

to find a place of our own and begin a normal married family life.

All was going well, until about one year on, when I started to have difficulty with the super bright light of the welding flash. It became impossible to weld, because my eyes fast streamed with water, so I went to my manager who arranged an immediate appointment with the hospital for tests.

When I asked the result, I was told that irritation, had caused conjunctivitis, "What's the cure?" I asked, "Change your job!" said the nurse chuckling.

Jobs were not easy to get in that area in the early 80s, so when I went home, Celia asked the result. When I explained, she went straight away and got the newspaper to look for a job. She said, "Nothing is worth losing your valuable sight for!"

I found an advert to train as a driving instructor and since I enjoyed being on the road, it was decided that we would contact the company. Two weeks later, I started my training, when our baby daughter was less than a week old!

With the birth of our second child, Sarah Joy, and my new job, life had changed dramatically and Celia and I spent less time together and even less time communicating. Time with Philip and Sarah was minimal and the officious, demanding side of my personality started to show through, which meant that I became a very dictatorial, hard father.

Philip was a typically active boy and was constantly surrounded by all his toys. One of the difficulties I always had was clutter and any untidiness.

This probably came from my being responsible for the state of the house when I was a child. The only one who did the piles of washing up that were left in horrible greasy water overnight was me! The only person to clear out the grate of ashes and light the fire was me!

I could go on but the reason for including this at this late stage and so many years on is to point out the way that those things of the past still held a power over the future. So, who got the venom? My kids, and of course, my precious wife Celia.

As far as the Driving Instructorship went, I was able to earn while I learned, and once I passed the first exam, of which there were three, I proceeded to become a fully qualified driving instructor, this whole process took about 16mths but I was able to start teaching within a couple of weeks.

I really enjoyed this way of life, which involved dealing with people on a one to one basis, which also gave me a great sense of satisfaction and for which I had a natural flair. So the position was ideal!

After another year, we decided to start our own school, because most of our business came from referrals, we worked out that we might as well work for ourselves and have the whole cake, rather than do the same thing for someone else and get only a small piece. This worked well and the 70+ hours I worked brought us in a good income.

The driving school had now grown to the point where no matter how hard I tried, there was no way that I could do all of the lessons on my own. So, we got another car and advertised for a trainee instructor. After several interviews, I decided on an ambitious lady instructor. That would give another dimension and angle to the school, so I started to train Pamela in the up to date methods of instruction.

To Have and To Hold

She had been an instructor years before and very soon showed that she got on well with the pupils and achieved good pass results. It seemed that my choice had been a good one, so both of us continued to grow the business and were soon both working long hours.

Since she was now bringing in new business, I did not want to lose her and possibly a large part of the driving school. Because this sort of thing often happened when partners left, we officially became business partners. We purchased a third car, firstly as a spare, secondly to start looking for another trainee.

Looking back, its easy to see how my life had gone from being God focused, to being more and more business focused. It's amazing, how making seemingly small decisions in our own strength, can be the beginning of a catastrophe. Sometimes, we can't tell the wood for the trees, we are blind to things that are obvious to someone looking on.

During all this time, I was in a battle with myself to make sense of what was going on inside. Who do we turn to when nothing you are thinking makes any sense? Who do we trust enough to open up all the things that have invaded our normally, peaceful, Christian life?

All the warning signs were there that I needed to talk to someone seriously about what was happening.

But who could I turn to when nothing I was thinking made any sense?

Who do we trust enough to open up all the things that have invaded our normally peaceful Christian life? It's at times of crisis, that we discover who we really know and trust. It's now that we perhaps question, "Who do I really know *that* well?" and probably as important, if not more so, "Who *really* knows me?"

Although I sought advice from men who I believed would be able to help me, they didn't fully appreciate what I was going through, so they just said, in effect "Pull yourself together!" They thought along with everyone else, (including myself) that I was a solidly based Christian, who was somehow above that kind of temptation.

I challenge you, the Reader, to find someone in your circle, to whom you can make yourself accountable; it will probably be the most important change that you will make for the rest of your life!

Everything in my seemingly ordered life was dropping apart and it was happening so fast, I couldn't cope! I knew all the things that I should do, but instead of doing them, I found myself on a slippery slope and as I stepped over the edge, everything gathered pace!

So what was happening? Firstly, Celia and I, through no fault of hers, were drifting apart, going through the motions of a supposed happy marriage; whilst my relationship with Philip and Sarah became one of a tyrant, rather than a father.

Due to the time I was spending with Pam, a relationship of mutual admiration, for our expertise as Driving Instructors, began to change, to a need to spend more and more time together.

The result was inevitable, unless I made a significant change, but I did not make that change, even though my lifestyle was obviously opposite to everything that I had held dear!

Reader, there is a serious warning here, meetings with the opposite sex, whether your marriage is secure or not, is likely to be the first step into wrong relationship. The outcome is almost inevitable.

By the end of August 1983, there was no way back! My life was totally in freefall! I was called in to see the elders and accused of adultery, which at that time had not physically taken place.

Because of my pride, I took the attitude that if I was going to be accused of an act, I might as well have the pleasure of it! So, at this point, I foolishly cut off my life line, my contact with people who truly loved and cared for me.

A few days later, I walked out on our marriage and left behind two beautiful children.

I went from there into rented accommodation, in a shared house, in one of the seedier parts of Nottingham. I continued to live a lie that lasted for the next sixteen years. From then on, all common sense went out of the window.

I suppose that like most of the people that I have spoken to, you are sitting there, saying, "How can a Father just walk out on two kids and his wife and not care?"

Well, I had to answer those questions myself and managed to find every excuse in the book. What I really did, was to rationalize, or to tell myself rational lies.

It's easy to find excuses for the thoughts, plans and actions we take. If we decide that is the direction we intend to go regardless of the consequences, then once set on course, nothing will deflect your plans.

So, with the guilt that I felt, I spent no time together with Celia, or the children. I never gave a real chance for there to be anything but a total breakdown of the whole family relationship. Inevitably we started moving toward divorce.

Chapter 21

The One who is left Behind

They were the words I had never thought I would ever hear, "I'm having an affair, and I'm enjoying it." I couldn't stay in our bed; instead, I spent an uncomfortable and restless night on the sofa, downstairs. My reply had been "I don't care how many women you have, I will always love you." But it had hurt, deeply and my stomach was in knots.

How had it come to this? I had thought that our marriage was a happy one? We had been married for 9 years by this time and after the excitement of constantly being on the move whilst Mike was in the army, we had finally settled down.

Philip was six and Sarah was now two and a half when Mike left. We had spent two and a half years in our first house, a deceptively large terrace house, before we saw a house for sale, which we believed God had reserved for us. It was an old Victorian Semi-detached house, with a large bay window, in a corner plot.

Mike and Celia Deakin

The sale went through very speedily, I only saw the house for the first time at New Year, but we had moved in before the middle of March. I often gave thanks to the Lord for that quick sale, because if it had dragged on, I could have been left in the other house (which was rather dark and dingy).

Mike could even have decided to sell the house and share the proceeds, (which weren't much) leaving me with no option but to live in a Council house. Very soon after this house prices and interest rates shot up and house sales were long drawn out processes for a couple of years. Evidence of God's perfect timing!

Our new house really felt like home to me. I loved it! We had a lovely sunny garden, and it was close to the local shops, so close, in fact, that I used to push the supermarket trolley home, so I never had to carry heavy shopping. Everything had seemed to drop into place.

We now had a lovely home, two lovely children, a good church, Mike had a job he enjoyed, and I was happy at home being a Wife and a Mum. Mike was still working long hours, but hey! Colic had only lasted 3 months and now Sarah was a happy 2 year old, and Philip was enjoying school. Yes, it seemed everything in the garden was coming up roses!

Even the Driving School was flourishing, we had taken on a lady instructor because there were lots of Asian girls who wanted to learn to drive, but their families wouldn't allow them to learn with a male instructor. This worked well for a few months, until she and her husband decided to move back to Wales.

I met Pam when she came for her Interview; I think Mike had already decided that she had got the job before she arrived. She seemed very pleasant and I had no reason to think that there would be any problems.

However, about a month or so later, they both arrived at the house to talk about a problem with her car. They decided go to the garage at the end of our road, and as I watched them walk together out of the gate, my heart did a lurch. Somehow, they looked too 'together', my first real indication that something was amiss.

A short time later, a friend of ours invited us round for a meal, we enjoyed the food she had prepared, but all evening Mike kept on saying "Pam this…" or "Pam that…" until I was fed up with listening to his conversation. When we got to bed that night, I asked him about it.

That's when he admitted, perhaps to himself as much as to me, that he was having an affair. It was probably more an affair of the heart at that time, which may have been why he asked me not to say anything to anyone.

However, when my friend, Jean, came to see me next morning, she found me in bits! My stomach so knotted

Mike and Celia Deakin

up, it was painful and as a close friend, it was impossible not to share what had taken place.

Mike was furious when he walked in unexpectedly and found Jean and I talking, and a few harsh words were exchanged. After he'd gone, Jean said I should talk to the elders but I decided not to take it any further, yet, and asked Jean to pray for us.

The next three months were a roller coaster for my emotions but through it all, I knew God's presence in a very deep and real way, like I'd never experienced before. There were times when I tried to pray for Mike, but all I could do was groan, "Oh, Lord, Mike!" and let the Spirit intercede for me! But, even in deep sorrow and despair, God would suddenly fill me with a joy that made me dance and sing! He gave me the strength to go on each day.

In late August, I took the children down to Sussex to visit my parents, and tried to act normally. Mike was going to decorate the through lounge, our main living area, not an easy task with two small children running around!

When I came home, it was to find the lounge half decorated, (it was a big room) Mike with a broken hand, where he had punched the wall?? He had also attempted to change the sheets on the bed, (obviously with only one hand) and had washed the one he'd taken off! I could see what I thought had happened, so I added two and two and made five! Mike denied anything had happened, but I decided it was time to go and see one of the Elders.

The tension just became tighter; I was so glad that I was able to talk to Jean. She and her husband, Andrew, were there for me whenever I needed them. One night, Mike came home and really tried to goad me, I got angry and started telling him a few home truths. He said, "You're really angry at me, that's a sin!"

"No!" I replied, "I'm not angry at you, I'm angry at Satan for what he's doing to you and to us, he's intent on ruining our lives!"

Mike went upstairs, and I paced the floor for a while, then I went out, and walked up to Jean's, the closest I came to walking out on him, but when I got there, the bedroom light was on, so I simply walked on round the block and came home.

Eventually, the day came that I had dreaded, Mike had threatened to leave and I had begged and pleaded with him to stay. Even in the early days of our marriage, if we had an argument, Mike would shout "I'm leaving!"

I never felt I had that option, not since the day I had gone home from Tidworth, with Anne driving, to collect the rest of our goods and chattels. Mum had said to me, "It's not too late you know, you can still leave him."

Mike and Celia Deakin

"But," I replied, "I don't want to leave him, why should you think I would want to leave? I love him, that's why I married him."

She said," Yes, but you haven't got any children yet."

I don't know what she saw in our relationship that bothered her, but I had only been married two or three months, and was blissfully happy. I had no idea of what might happen in the future, I had married for life, and neither of us believed in divorce, so I was shocked that my Mother should even be suggesting such a thing!

Life together had not always been easy, but we had come through and resolved many issues with The Lords' help. Now, I was devastated, that he should want to leave! How would I cope on my own with two children? What effect would it have on their young lives? It was like living through a nightmare! I couldn't really believe that it was happening!

The day before he left, he calmly collected all his shirts and pressed them, packed all his clothes and went to bed. The next morning, he picked up his bag, gave me a kiss on the cheek and walked out of the door. That was on October 14th 1983.

Strangely enough, (and I've found this to be a principal) when the thing I had dreaded actually happened, it wasn't as bad as I'd feared. Suddenly, all the tension was released, like a balloon when you let it go without tying it up!

To Have and To Hold

I phoned Jean, and then I phoned Dave, the Elder. He asked me if I could arrange for him to speak to Pam. She agreed to come and see Dave. I don't really remember what was said, now, but nothing was resolved, and I believe she denied any wrong doing or inciting Mike to leave home.

Mike moved into a caravan on a static site, and a couple of weeks later, I took the children down to Exeter, to visit our friends, Gwen and Peter. When I came back, I found Mike had moved back in for the time I was away. He came back to see me, to explain and said, "I'm willing to come back home."

So, I said, "I have forgiven you for what is past but if you come back, you must stop seeing Pam, and she must stop working for/with you."

His reply was "I'm only willing to come back on my terms. I want Pam to continue with the driving school."

"Well," I replied, "in that case, you had better not come back until God has dealt with you. Then you can come back!"

I had already gone through enough, and I didn't want to be part of a love triangle. It had to be all or nothing! In the meantime, I was ready to sit it out!

I didn't tell the children he had gone, (they were only six and two and a half) as I still hoped that Mike would see sense and come home. He had been going out early in

Mike and Celia Deakin

the morning and not returning until late at night. Philip and Sarah didn't know what was happening; all they knew was that Daddy was working very late.

It wasn't till very much later that Philip found out that Daddy wasn't living with us. Sarah knew, because she would often crawl into my bed. I used to laugh and say "Weeping endureth for a night, but (Sarah) Joy cometh in the morning!"

Chapter 22

The Promise

Life began to settle into a more normal pattern, but people at church still didn't really know what was happening. They only knew that Mike was no longer going to church, which indicated that there was a problem.

About seven weeks after Mike had left home, Andrew told the prayer group that Mike had left home and suggested a week of prayer and fasting. At one of the prayer sessions that I managed to attend, the Lord brought to mind the story of King Nebuchadnezzar and his dream of the tree, from Chapter 4 of the Book of Daniel.

Briefly, in the dream, Nebuchadnezzar sees a huge oak tree, supporting all kinds of wild life, then an angel gives the order for the tree to be cut down, but to leave the stump and roots in the earth banded with a brass and iron chain. Daniel tells the King that the dream is a warning to him to rule in mercy, but the King doesn't heed the warning. A year later, the King is proudly looking around at his kingdom, when he is struck down with a form of insanity, and for seven years, he lives in the field, eating grass, with long hair, like eagles' feathers and nails like birds' claws.

At the end of seven years, his understanding returns to him, and he looks up and praises the God of Heaven. He is restored to all his former glory and kingdom and was re-established with even greater honour than before!

I took this as a promise from God, that He would restore Mike, how long that would take, I had no idea, but, at a time when everything was crashing around my ears, the one certainty in my life was, that God would never let me down.

I clung to Him as the one solid, immovable thing in my life, the one person on whom I could depend; who I knew was utterly faithful. He was, and is and will forever be, my rock and hiding place, as King David found and so often wrote in the Psalms, such as in the 91st Psalm.

As the Word for Today was to put it years later:

"The Law of Progression had begun.

"Unless a corn of wheat falls into the ground and dies, it abides alone, but if it dies it will bring forth much fruit, some 30 fold, some 60 fold and some 100 fold."

John Ch12:v24

> ***"First the blade, then the ear, after that the full corn in the ear."***
>
> *Mark Ch 4: v28*

I was in the "I don't know season." My seed was in the ground, but I was in the dark. The how and when was up to God…..all I knew was, SOMEDAY IT WILL come to pass!"

Now, Christmas was not too far away, and I still hadn't told my parents anything about what was happening! At first, knowing that mum and dad didn't have a particularly high opinion of Mike; I didn't want to scupper Mike's chances of reconciliation. Then Mum got Shingles and was quite poorly, so I didn't want to put her under any stress, and now, I didn't want to ruin their Christmas.

So, we got through Christmas, Mike arrived with some presents for the children and a carriage clock for me. ("So I could count the minutes I spent alone?" I thought). He spent much of the day with us, but relations were strained, as they say!

After New Year, I phoned Mum and Dad, and asked if we could come down for a couple of days to see them. I had something I wanted to discuss with them.

Once the children were in bed, I sat down with my parents and told them the whole sorry tale. It was possibly the hardest thing I had to do, it was like admitting defeat, but I couldn't put it off any longer.

Another hard thing was to go to the DHSS Office and ask for a handout, such an impersonal, bleak, hopeless kind of place, ughhh! I also had to go to the Bank Manager, and close our Joint account. He was just so kind and sympathetic, that I found myself in floods of tears. What would I be like when I had to go to the Solicitor to arrange the Separation Order? Not as bad as I thought, as she was very matter-of-fact and professional and I found I was ok.

Mike used to come to the house to see the children, for about an hour or so around Sunday teatime. It was very difficult for us all; Mike was trying to be interested, caring daddy, but was also trying to discipline them, which just made them very upset. I had to sit and watch and make a little conversation, which was difficult. Then, because he had to go, the children would get clingy and upset, which would upset me. Then some weeks he didn't come at all!

In the end, I told him, "I want you to continue seeing the children; I think it's important, but either you come regularly or not at all, or you arrange to take them out. So, he just stopped coming, and we very rarely heard from him.

To Have and To Hold

Somehow, I got through that first year, (always the hardest!). It was like loosing my right arm, or like bereavement, but there was no closure to the situation. With bereavement, yes sometimes there are regrets, but there are also happy memories, with separation and divorce, those are lost, somehow.

I had plenty of time for regrets. I went over everything in my mind, again and again. Did I make the right decision when Mike asked to come back, but on his terms? Could I have done things differently? Had I jumped to the wrong conclusion about what happened while Mike was decorating?

Eventually, I told Philip, that his Daddy was running away from God, and that was why he no longer lived with us. Together we would pray for him, every day, at first, but later, I let it drop, because the constant reminder was upsetting for the children.

Yes, I still loved him, but in the same way that you might love a distant cousin or uncle. That was the only way. I couldn't live with a passionate, unrequited love in the long term. I think I would have become a nervous wreck!

Mum and Dad had been great. Yes, there were a lot of negative opinions voiced about Mike, and his treatment of me, but they had rallied round me and gave me a great deal of support, throughout the whole time I was on my own.

Mike said he wanted a divorce, but I felt that his impulsive nature needed time to cool its heels. The law then, was, that if one party didn't agree to the divorce, then it could only go through after 5 years' separation. I told him he would have to wait for the full 5 years.

A year after we separated, I was able to say, "Well, I've made it through the first year, so I guess I'll make it through to the end!" After another year, I'd decided that if Mike wanted a divorce, he could have one.

I was beginning to rediscover who I was! I finished decorating the Lounge, and then decorated my bedroom. Thus began the process of making my house a home and the start of a lasting passion for interior design.

Chapter 23
Life with Pam

When I had left Celia it didn't take long for me to realise that life with Pam was not going to be an easy ride. She already had two young children with another man. They were beautiful kids but were hopelessly spoilt, it didn't matter what they wanted they got it. Sally and Stewart were not used to ever being told no; this became a major issue between Pam and I and started a situation that was to continue throughout the whole of our time together.

Soon after us getting together we realised that we could not function as a couple at home and at work, so I left Pam to continue to run the existing school and went to work for another company. This really didn't work either so it was mutually decided that the answer was for me to find a different occupation, completely outside of driving schools. So after looking in the papers, I made an application to an Insurance company as what is called a tied agent, which means that I could only offer policies from one company.

Having made an appointment with the company I was called into the first of two interviews. This consisted of a psychometric test, which enables the company to assess a person's attitude, aptitude, opinions and suitability for the position; through questions and answers which at the time seemed as though they didn't make sense.

It was not possible to find out if I was successful on this first interview because the papers had to go away to be checked. But I met the district manager who I felt very comfortable with. He came over as a competent, friendly, and approachable person. His name was Liam; I knew that I could work easily with this man if I was offered the position. Only time would tell.

I was waiting eagerly for the next few days for a letter or for the phone to ring. Eventually, the call came; I had been short listed to a second interview.

Looking back I would have done things differently had I known more, but when I turned up I had just finished a driving lesson. It was a beautiful warm, sunny day! I was wearing a short sleeved red and white striped shirt with an open neck, cream coloured trousers and cream moccasin shoes. I was sporting a beard and moustache which made me look like the Yorkshire ripper!

I went in for another test and having finished went to wait for my interview with Liam. While I was waiting I got into conversation with a guy called Roy who was the epitome of the typical insurance salesman. Dripping with gold, Rolex watch, a suit that you would cut you hand on the sharpness of the crease, greased back hair and the 'must have' bright red tie! It was at this point that I realised this made what I was wearing, the least like a salesman that I could possibly be!

Roy said "That is what you want to aim for, if you come on board". He was pointing at a poster advertising a free holiday to Orlando Florida, based on achieving a certain target on sales. The door opened and I was summoned into the interview.

Liam said that he was very pleased with the results of both of the tests. "What would you like to earn in the next twelve months, if we offered you a position?" he queried. At the time, my net pay was about £7,500 for a 70 hour week, so my reply was that I would like to double this.

He leaned forward as he asked "What would you like to achieve this year, outside of money?" I remembered the poster in the office and said, "I want to be on that trip to Florida, do you think I could do that?" I asked.

"If you will give the same commitment and dedication to this position, you will laugh at £15000! But you should also know that it has never been done by a rank amateur before!"

What a challenge! Anyway he offered me the position and booked me in to start the rigorous training. The one thing I had never been afraid of was hard work!

Before leaving his office Liam gently pointed out to me the inappropriate nature of the clothes I was wearing. I made a pledge to Liam and to myself that I would never be caught out like that again and I never was!

During and after the training, Liam became my first and most important mentor, not just with regard to work but also as a father figure in tough situations! During the time I was with the company I made sure that I not only reached but exceeded any and all targets I was given!

It seemed that over the next few years that the harder I worked the more the family spent; the more money I provided the more they wanted! Here I was on the one hand achieving goals that I would never have believed possible, with a lifestyle where no one could have asked for more but the family were never satisfied. By 1989 the relationship with Pam had begun a downward slide;

To Have and To Hold

it became a three against one situation with me being that one.

Pam became insanely jealous and began accusing me of all sorts of things, none of which were justified, nor did I have time or inclination for them. At this point it was decided that in order to give Pam and the children a feeling of security that we should get married.

Let's review the situation for this forthcoming marriage. I was working like a Trojan to satisfy the wants of an insatiable family, we were arguing and fighting on an almost a daily basis, my intended wife-to-be shared none of my dreams and aspirations and would not allow me any say in the running or control of the home or children. How stupid can you be and still claim to have a brain?

This whole situation was obviously a recipe for disaster from the very start; but not for the first time it was as though my head was on back to front! Inside, I knew all along that there was no way that such a relationship could last but didn't know what else to do, which made me feel emasculated. I agreed to things that I would never normally have given a second thought, yet I did them.

Life became heavier as the months and years passed, with the hours I was working to keep up with the spending and the ongoing bills. Pam became more jealous and we were consequently always arguing. This was no good to Pam, the children or me and it was only a matter of time before the bubble would burst!

Just after we were married we decided that we should move house and area, which we did, this was the beginning of a catalogue of disaster both emotionally and financially.

We purchased a beautiful bungalow that was in a really pretty village on the edge of Nottinghamshire. The setting was idyllic but putting the surroundings in order doesn't do anything to change relationships, even though that was part of the reason for the change. As I intimated everything in the garden was not rosy.

I decided about this time that I was going to take up the offer of a new position which was too good to miss. I was head hunted to go to a health care organization and set up a financial services arm to provide mortgages, loans and insurance and pensions to that sector.

The move I made was for nothing more than an enormous ego, with that worst of all sins, pride. The company were offering me a really good package, too good to be true, some would say!

One of the things which unfortunately I have only learned by bitter experience, is that if it sounds too good to be true it most probably is! This opportunity lasted precisely four months until the parent company went bankrupt, leaving me well and truly in the mire.

For any of you who have been in this situation the signs are obvious, if you know what to look for. Huddles of accountants sat talking in whispers, not answering the phone calls, but me? I was as green as the grass.

I hadn't a clue what was going on, until the day that I arrived to be greeted by the company lawyer.

Since I was the Chairman of the financial services company, I was advised to write out my resignation, to avoid any responsibility for what was about to happen.

I was to leave the car keys, mobile phone and office keys and walk away. No! I probably wouldn't get any of the 60K plus commission and fees I had worked for! Just walk away.

When I got home there was an eruption, telling me how short sighted, arrogant and stupid I had been. Just the sort of support I needed! I was already feeling lower than a snake's belly, but that was the way Pam dealt with it!

Within the next twelve months, the serious situation was to become like a black comedy. When I had left Cannon I had left behind a 250 person client list which would have guaranteed me a healthy living for as long as I had a need for one. Instead I was now unemployed, with a large new mortgage and a relationship in chaos and that was just the beginning.

It was at this time that we found out that the solicitor we had used (a business colleague) had actually not paid the funds for the purchase into the appropriate accounts and had run off with the money! This meant that the owner was not paid therefore we did not own the property.

We had ordered and had a new conservatory added to the rear of the house. This had been incorrectly built and was leaking through the roof and through the walls onto live electricity cables! The soil from the foundations had been shovelled up against the outside of the conservatory to a height of two feet above the damp course. So the company were threatening us with physical injury because we were obviously not going to pay for this shambles until it was completed! Well, shambles just about sums up the situation!

So, I now redoubled my efforts, to get a job that would pay the bills, until the mess was sorted out. By 1995 the situation was still in chaos but I had become the eternal optimist; so I went to work in a double-glazing company, working seven days a week, twelve-sixteen hours minimum, each day to try to rectify the mess.

Despite all of the faults which I already told you of, there was a part of me that was definitely *not* Mr. Average. No matter what was going to happen, due to the input of dozens of Self Improvement books and tapes I had a positive mental attitude; I was not going down without a fight!

They were the only thing that kept me sane during this time and were a constant source of encouragement as I drove the thousands of miles that were necessary to fulfil my appointments, about 1500 mile a week.

It was starting to tell on me. I became very nervous, but managed to hide this at work by constantly having a book to read, or being out on appointments with clients; somehow I managed to keep a stiff upper lip appearance and maintained a positive, professional attitude.

After two years I knew I couldn't keep up this pace and stay sane or in control. I avoided going home in order to avoid the arguments and I literally slept in the car in lay-by's or car parks, so what was the answer?

Divorce? Give away all that I'd paid for?

I knew that a divorce from Pam would not be an easy one due to the lack of any relationship between us. This was going to be messy and very painful, anyway having been divorced before, this one was an easier decision to make, (how sad!) But being honest, I saw no other choice, if I was to survive.

At the end of the year I left home and moved away from the area to avoid the threatened beatings from one of Pam's relations. In total Pam and I had been together for just over twelve years and to be fair, most of that time was spent in a conflict situation.

By 1997 the decree absolute became final and that was the last time that I ever saw Pam.

Chapter 24

Celia Moving On

After a couple of years, I was feeling much more settled and the children and I, were beginning to enjoy life. I started helping out at a Christian café, just one morning a week. It gave me a chance to meet other people and enjoy some grown up company!

During this time, I heard that Mike had married Pam, they invited Philip to go out with them for a meal to celebrate, but I certainly didn't feel like celebrating! Where was God in all this? Had I heard wrongly? Perhaps, God had only meant that He would restore Mike to Himself, and not to me? It knocked my confidence somewhat, and I was glad that I had friends around me to support and encourage me.

One of the people who came into the café, was an Irishman, I used to get him talking, just so I could listen to his beautiful, lilting accent! As I got to know him, I found him very easy to talk to, and the conversation flowed

Mike and Celia Deakin

very easily. I discovered that he had lived a fascinating life and was a great story teller.

One lunch time, he offered me a lift home, as he was going my direction. In conversation on the way home, he asked if I had any plans for the afternoon. I replied that I had to deliver my Avon orders to my customers. He parked the car in the car park, which was opposite my house, and we stood chatting for a while, before he left to go to the Bank.

I went indoors, feeling rather shaken. What would have happened if I'd not had anything planned? Was he about to invite me to go for a ride with him? I hadn't even realised that it might have been a loaded question, and had answered it quite naturally and honestly. I was glad that God had kept me from making a move I knew I would regret.

However, the seed thought took root, and soon I was day dreaming about him, true, he wasn't good looking, but looks weren't everything. There was just one problem; he was happily married, with two children. I knew I couldn't put them through what I had been through!

I battled with my feelings and emotions, but over the next few weeks I didn't see him. He never came near the café. Had he seen the danger signals, too? I thought he must have done.

Then one Saturday, I popped into the bookshop and he was there. On impulse, I invited him and his wife and family to come to dinner with us the following day. The meal passed off smoothly enough and we spent a pleasant afternoon together. It did the trick, seeing him in the context of his family served to drive all wrong thoughts straight out of the window! I only saw him once after that, at a Summer Fete with all his family.

God gives us the grace to do the right thing, but it is a matter of the will and not the heart. I had learned a valuable lesson; I was vulnerable to attack from Satan and needed to guard against temptation.

In September 1988, I started working Night duty at a local Nursing home, just two or three nights a week. My friend's daughter came to baby-sit, and get the children up and ready for school. I would cycle home and go to bed.

I stayed there, till the following spring, the work was quite heavy and I was the only trained nurse on duty, with two care assistants. The problem was, I ended up by only getting about 5 or 6 hours sleep, before the children were home and bouncing all over me!

It was all extra hassle and I found I was not coping with the children very well. I was tired and short-tempered and since I was only coming out with about £10.00 extra a week, I called it quits.

Mike and Celia Deakin

I moved to another Home and worked Days, driving a Three Wheeler, Reliant car. That job only lasted a few weeks, as the car I had bought turned out to be unroadworthy, and I had to have a car to reach the Home.

While I was working at the second home, Mike and a colleague came to the house to ask me a favour. He said he needed a loan and would I be willing to take out a re-mortgage on the house for £10,000. He promised that he would pay it off and everything would be fine. (He used some emotional blackmail on me, really, as I realised later.)

Anyway, I agreed, and he asked me not to tell anyone else. It all went through, and the cheque for £10,000 arrived. I phoned him to let me know, and he asked me to meet him a short way from our house. I put it in my bag, and rode to meet him on my bike. He was in quite a flash car and it seemed incongruous that here was I on a bike giving him a hefty cheque!!?

That evening, Keith, one of our elders, phoned me to see how I was, He suddenly said, "Oh, by the way, have you heard from Mike? How's his financial situation? Do you know?" I found myself telling him what had happened. His voice was suddenly urgent, "Celia, you've got to stop that cheque, first thing in the morning! STOP THAT CHEQUE!!" I was shaking as I put down the

To Have and To Hold

phone with the words still ringing in my ears, "STOP THAT CHEQUE!!!"

I was supposed to be at work in the morning, so I phoned and told them something very urgent had come up that I had to deal with. They weren't pleased, nor was Mike, when he discovered what I had done, later that day, but again, I believe it was evidence of God's hand looking after me.

Anyway, I left the job soon afterwards, and got involved in organising a Summer Play scheme for the local children. It went off very well, and a good time was had by all.

About a year later, I started a typing course, it was only one day a week, but it was a start. The following year when Sarah was in year 6, I started a full-time Mature Secretarial course, at a local college. I'm afraid I never did become a proficient Touch Typist but I did learn Word Processing and how to use all my fingers!

I completed the course and surprised myself by achieving an RSA II in typing. (The standard is very high, due to a very tiny margin for error!) The course finished in July, so I spent the summer with the children, before looking for a job in September.

Chapter 25

Family Life

Every summer, we went to a Christian Conference, at Rora, near Newton Abbot in Devon. We always went by train, and stayed in a tent for the week. We met up with all our friends and the children were free to run and play with children they had met on previous years!

Philip's birthday usually fell during that week, on the same day as the Queen Mothers' birthday, so he celebrated his birthday with his "Rora" friends.

We would hire a tent and air beds, blankets and tables, chairs and cooker. But of course, it still left loads of camping equipment, to be packed and carried between us! There were at least two changes of train in each direction, but somehow we managed it.

One journey we never forgot was in 1990, it had been a scorcher of a week! When we reached the Station at Newton Abbot, the newspaper headlines were all about the temperature reaching 90° on the Queen Mother's 90th birthday!

To Have and To Hold

We boarded the train, but soon discovered that the air conditioning was not working in our compartment and the windows were not made to open! We sat there, feeling like we were being boiled alive!

Unfortunately for British Rail, there was a man on the train whose job was to monitor Customer Satisfaction!! This he did, by enthusiastically interviewing every one in our compartment! What a pity British Rail hadn't brought in a system of compensation for inconvenience at that time. It should, at least, have been worth a year of free travel!!

We also regularly travelled down to Sussex to see my Mum and Dad. Sarah had the ability to make friends with someone on every trip, perhaps a young lady on the train or the tube, or a Dutch family who had been sightseeing in London. She chatted to them all and would exchange addresses so they could send her friendship bracelets or something similar.

Philip, too, was not backwards in coming forward! (if you know what I mean?). They had a lot of confidence and seemed to instinctively know who they could trust.

At the time they were growing up, there was a lot of emphasis on the "Say no to Strangers" campaign, and although I taught them the principals behind it, I also allowed them to be themselves. I didn't want to destroy their outgoing, sunny, friendly natures' by filling them

Mike and Celia Deakin

with fear. Now they are grown up, I know I did the right thing, as I see Philip's children with the same open–ness and spontaneity!

It wasn't always easy to bring them up. Philip is very similar to me in personality, although he grew up to look and sound a lot like his Dad. Sarah looks more like me, but is very much like her Dad, with a very strong will, outgoing, charming and lots of fun!

Philip, I could handle, as I understood him and we became great friends as he grew older. We would sit and talk animatedly for hours, bouncing off each other, and covering a vast range of subjects.

Sarah was a very different kettle of fish! At the age of 4 years, she seemed to withdraw from me, as though subconsciously she blamed me for the loss of her Dad. When she reached her teens, she withdrew to the safety of her room, and spent much of her time there.

It was only after Philip left home, that Sarah and I really started to get along better. I was always aware that I really needed Mike there as father, to handle her, because I knew he would understand the way she ticked.

We still went to the House Church Fellowship, which had long since outgrown the house and had bought their own building. One of the buildings they had been offered had been the local Mortuary! There were many jokes flying around about possible names for the church; as in: - The

New Life Church… The Church of the Resurrection….or St Lazarus!! You get the idea! But it didn't have sufficient parking space, so wasn't approved. Pity!

Most of the founder members of the church had moved into Nottingham from other areas, so it became quite a fluid congregation, who were prepared to move elsewhere for work.

Many of the people I was closest to moved away, Keith and Dave and their families; John and Anne, who we had stayed with when we first came to Nottingham; all moved to take up leadership roles in other churches or Fellowships. Even Jean and Andrew moved away, just as Sarah and their youngest, Luke, were about to start senior school.

When Dave and Judith left, their place as leaders was filled by Martin and Helen. Right from the start, they seemed to take us to their hearts and we loved them, too! Martin joined Keith and Andrew in helping to provide a father figure particularly for Philip but also for Sarah.

The Fellowship became our family, in a very real sense. We were often invited to various homes for Sunday lunch. Often, there were Christmas gifts for us all, plus envelopes containing anonymous gifts of cash, for me to cover unexpected bills, or to buy those little extras! Yes, we were blessed indeed!

Mike and Celia Deakin

In many ways, I had been able to put the hurts of the past behind me, but there were times of poignancy, when I hurt for my children, and what they were missing.

Chapter 26

A New Career?

September came, and I now embarked on what I thought was to be my new career as a typist/word processor operator. I applied for many jobs, but didn't get anywhere! I didn't realise how quickly you loose your speed at typing, when you don't practise. Nor did I realise that most employers take little notice of your qualifications! That just gets you the interview!

Time after time, I was placed in front of a strange typewriter, or a word processor with a different program to the one I had learned, and asked to take a speed test. I ended up a bag of nerves and flunked the tests, the more interviews I attended, the worse I got! If only they had given me a chance to settle in and gain my confidence in the work situation?

At the end of October, I was offered a clerical job, in a Quantity Surveyors office, dealing with Bills of Quantity. This mainly entailed doing reams and reams of photocopying, on a huge machine, so that I could send the copies out to various companies, with an invitation to tender a price for the job, as specified. I actually enjoyed the job, and started making friends.

At Christmas time, all of the Construction industry closes down for two weeks, so I was able to enjoy time with the children. On returning to work after New Year, there was a sense of unease in the office.

We soon found out the reason, one of the Banks that had been keeping the Company's head above water was recalling its loan. We were heading for Receivership. Even though we had orders on the books, the Bank was either too short-sighted, or too impatient to wait any longer.

We were ok, we had been paid before Christmas, but I felt sorry for all the Contractors and Sub-Contractors, who would probably come out with nothing!

So, it was back to the job centre, again. After taking a couple of "Temping" positions, I eventually found a job as a Filing Clerk, with Laing Management. They were working on a highly innovative project in town, constructing the new Inland Revenue Centre.

I say innovative, because all the parts of the building were being made in a local concrete factory, to very high specification. These were then transported to the site, where they simply fitted them together like Lego bricks! They were also doing all the Quantity Surveying as they were building and receiving Tenders for the next task on almost a day to day basis.

It was a very fast pace in the office, and I often had to answer the phone. I found it hard when they called, to catch people's names, whilst also registering who they wished to speak to! I was being asked to do switchboard work, really, for which I had no experience.

The Boss was a Christian and was very well respected (he didn't allow any swearing in the office) and was fair in all his dealings. Eventually, he called me into his office and told me that I wasn't up to the job; he also said that he'd never met anyone quite like me, before! I could only guess that he meant I was not at all business minded!? I was obviously a square peg in a round hole!

I went back to the Job Centre, and the Temping agencies. Really, Temping is all right if you are an experienced, good all-rounder, but for someone like me, I never quite found my feet, and struggled every inch of the way. I really did try to make a "go" of office work, but really, it wasn't me.

It was now October, 1993, and I applied to work in Debenhams, as a Sales Consultant (Shop Assistant) for the Christmas period. I was accepted, and started on the Home Department. I loved it, it was exciting, there were people to talk to, and I found it really interesting!

Mike and Celia Deakin

The job finished at New Year, but I kept on badgering the Personnel Department to give me a job. In February, I was offered a part-time temporary position on Coloroll, till July. Then I moved onto a new Haberdashery Concession. In June 1995, I went on a holiday with Oak Hall to Tuscany in Italy! It was wonderful, I really enjoyed it, despite being older than most of my travelling companions, it somehow didn't matter. We were all Christians and shared some memorable times, together!

On my return, I discovered that the haberdashery firm had become victims of the downturn in Home Dressmaking, and were going into receivership within the week!

However, our Personnel Manager promised to find us all jobs in Store, and within two days, I was working for a Jewellery Concession, downstairs. I reported on the Thursday morning for half a day's training with the Manageress, Bela and the Area Manageress, Julie. Everything went well, they were both very friendly, and I was sure that I would enjoy working there.

At around midday, Julie took her leave, to go on to another store. As soon as she had gone, Bela turned to me, "I am feeling very sick, I must go home. You'll be alright to take over, won't you?"

"Yes, I'll manage, don't worry." I said, wondering if I'd been set up, like on those TV Shows!

"The girls on the other jewellery counters will help if you need to know anything. Here's the keys!" And with that she was gone! I was in sole charge for the next five days!

I continued to work with them for about 20 months, and really enjoyed a new sense of confidence. When, a few months later, Bela took a month's holiday in India, I found that I loved being able to run the concession and felt that I had at last found my niche!

Chapter 27

The Times they are a'changin'

It was during this time, that Philip had felt the need to find fellowship with people of his own age group. He had struggled to find his own faith, and eventually decided to commit his life to Jesus, and was duly baptised in a skip at a baptism service at Rora. Friends at college had invited him to join them at "T" Street as The Christian Centre was affectionately known, situated as it was on Talbot Street.

He didn't know what to expect, but came home very excited! "Wow, Mum!" he said, "There were so many young people there, I was gobsmacked!" We always used to say that Philip had "More Rabbit than Sainsbury's!" So, for Philip to be speechless, I knew it had to be something big!

A couple of months later, Phil invited me to the Christmas Production at "T" Street. It was very impressive. In a large hall, which I later found out would seat 600, we were treated to a very professional, production

To Have and To Hold

with excellent singers, using multi media to put over the Christmas message. However, it wasn't the slick style or anything like that, but the sense of God's presence that impressed me most.

I started going to "T" Street on Sunday evenings, in February 1996, but felt like I was only "toe dipping"! In such a large church, it was necessary to dive right in.

I had felt dissatisfied at the Fellowship for quite some time, and I was just "going through the motions." Even Helen and Martin had left, to go abroad as missionaries. I had felt hemmed in, what the Bible called "Hedged about"! I longed to escape but didn't know how.

Suddenly, God seemed to be opening up a door of opportunity for me. So eager was I to grasp it, that I began comparing the two churches (never a good idea!). I had always been quite radical in my views, but in order to fit in, had reined them in, but now, I definitely had the bit between my teeth and I was going for it!

In an open letter to the Congregation, I gave full rein to some of my long held grievances, and basically told them to "Get with it". (This practice of slamming the door behind you is definitely NOT to be recommended!) Derek, the Elder, came to se me, I apologised, and on my last Sunday, apologised to the whole church, but, the damage had been done, and people had been hurt. After

Mike and Celia Deakin

all their kindness down through the years, it was not a good way to say goodbye.

A few months later, I had a phone call one evening from a very distraught Pam. "Celia," she said, "Mike says he's leaving me! How did you cope, when he left you?"

"I put my trust in Jesus." I replied. "Oh," she wailed, "My mother told me that if he could leave one marriage, he could more easily leave a second partner! And she was right, I should have listened!"

I suggested that she should seek for advice from her local Pentecostal church, and said I would pray for her.

I put down the phone with mixed feelings. I felt for her distress, and I prayed that she would find answers to her situation. On the other hand, I had always felt that Mike had been almost spellbound by Pam, and this was the first signal that the spell was, at last, broken! ***Just like the first green blade of corn, is the signal of things to come!*** But as James exhorted his readers,

"Be patient, like a farmer who waits until the autumn for his precious harvest to ripen."

James Ch 5 v 7

I was invited to join a single group, called Great Nights!" Run by a married couple from "T" Street, it counted amongst its members, people from many different churches around the greater Nottingham area. At first, there were just evening events, but later walks in Derbyshire and other daytime events were also arranged.

I went along, not so much to find a partner, as to have company to go out with. Churches are generally made up of family groups, children's activities, youth/student groups and twilight groups. Sadly, today, there are many people who don't fit into any of these; people who have come through traumatic relationship breakdowns and are bruised and hurting, or people (mostly women) who have never found that Mr Right.

We enjoyed some good times with good company, sometimes sharing how God had brought us out of our circumstances, giving hope to those who were still struggling!

Some years before, Dad had paid for me to have double glazing fitted to my house, and now I felt was a good time to get some other improvements done. With the help and encouragement of the church financial advisor, I applied for a Re-mortgage. I had a shower fitted, and ordered a new kitchen. I also decided to go on a Special Paint Effects, Interior Design Course at a local Design Academy. I had seen a ready to paint, self style kitchen, and planned to decorate it myself.

In the new year of 1997, Debenhams had commenced an extended period of major refurbishment of the

Nottingham store. It had originally been around six shops, which had been knocked into one store. At one side those shops had been on a steep hill, so, it was said, there were around 43 different floor levels within the store.

When our Jewellery Concession realised just how much mess and dirt was flying around and saw the poky corner position they had moved us into, they decided they would pull out until the refurbishment was completed.

So it was, that once more, I found myself without a job, totally unexpectedly, the week before I was due to start the Course, which was the same week my kitchen was due to be ripped out!! It was now Friday, far too late to cancel everything, so I just went ahead with my plans.

The two guys arrived on Monday morning to do the kitchen, as I left to start my course! They must have worked like Trojans, because it was all completed by Saturday afternoon! A blank canvas for me to paint!

I had really enjoyed the Course, where we learned a technique by watching an expert, then practising and completing a sample board of each paint effect, to show potential customers! In all, we covered nearly 70 modules over the course of the week. These included the basics of colour spectrums, and preparation of surfaces and how to cost for a project, as well as learning to do marbling, rag rolling, gilding, stencilling, crackle glazing and the all important Hand Painted Kitchen!

This then was to be my project, for the next five weeks, before commencing part two of the Course. Any writer or artist will tell you that this is a scary moment, faced with a blank sheet of paper, or canvas! Like infinity, it stretches out in all directions, and you somehow have to pin it down.

So, it's actually easier, when there is already something in the room as a base or anchor, like a chair, carpet or picture, because you have a starting point.

I painted the kitchen units a lovely pale lavender blue, and then rag rolled the panels in a slightly deeper blue, purple and white. I also painted the fridge/freezer, washing machine and dishwasher, to match, and finished with three coats of varnish.

The end wall was blank and needed something. I had wanted to put a patio door in it, but I couldn't afford to do that. Instead, I painted an archway and prepared to paint a view.

Phil had been on a Leadership Course held at "T" Street, which finished in June. At the End-of-Course Service, one of the graduates, Dennis, was talking about the story of the raising of Jairus' daughter, from the dead. He said, "There are those of you, here, who have promises which God gave you, perhaps many years ago, but you've

Mike and Celia Deakin

still not seen them fulfilled. Like Jairus' daughter, they seem to you to be dead, but they are only sleeping!"

So, like Jairus' daughter, those promises were awakened, by faith

Meanwhile, God was at work!

At the end of August 1997, I had a phone call from Mike; he wanted to come over to see the children. Philip was now taller than his dad and Sarah was growing up, too! On the day he came, they had both gone to a friends' wedding at "T" Street, so he came in and sat down at the breakfast bar and chatted to me for about an hour, while we waited for them to return.

He seemed very relaxed and confident, as he explained that the reason he had not seen very much of the children while he was with Pam, was because she was very jealous and it caused many rows. He had simply taken the route of least resistance! We enjoyed a pleasant time, in each others company.

Phil and Sarah arrived back, and I asked Phil to go and buy a film for the camera, so I could take some photo's of them with their Dad. I was surprised when Mike offered to take a picture of me with the children, before taking them out to a Chinese restaurant.

So, I saw another green blade of corn, a tiny blade of encouragement that the answer was on its way!

Chapter 28

Mike Meets Penny

During this time I met a young lady who I fell head over heels in love with, we hit it off on the first meeting, time seemed to stand still and we seemed to draw out the best in each other.

Apart from my early marriage to Celia, I had never met anyone who totally engaged my attention and admiration as she did. Everything that a woman could have was present, inner and outer beauty, style, panache, sense of humour, true elegance and a sense of going somewhere.

At first I was totally in awe, which sometimes made me feel inferior, later I was able to see how well we complemented each others strong and weak points.

As the winter snows came down, we took long drives out into the country; we found our own special place on the other side of the bridge, that's the Humber Bridge in Lincolnshire.

To Have and To Hold

One night we set off at about 11o'clock to go over the bridge, we went down to the marina and parked the car. It was a sharp moonlit evening, all the stars had come out to light the way, as we got out of the car we both set off running towards the edge of the marina, we were like two giddy little kids on our first date.

Although we had spent so much time together, this was the first time we had felt like this, I wanted to grab her hand and run with her but I was afraid it would break the magic of the moment; so far we had just been friends and companions.

Both of us had broken relationships but we hadn't thought of each other in that way.

As we reached the edge we reached out for each other's hand and just continued to stare at the beautiful surroundings, it was so good to share this time.

From this time on how wonderful my life felt, all the cuddly things that go with the typical story of two people in love were happening, note cards, flowers, love notes, hours on the phone and just being together.

Starting to talk of the future, my life, our lives were starting to gather momentum and as it went on so our love and respect for each other grew.

We went away to New York for a Christmas break and enjoyed the festive atmosphere. I was introduced to the theatre for the first time on Broadway and learned to love the arts, music, theatre, opera, balls, all became part of my life.

What a full life we began to live, I had learned from the past that doing normal things together was also an important part of a balanced life.

Suddenly, my life was fully of excitement, fun, laughter and love, we revelled in each other and in everything we did! Even a trip to the supermarket was exiting and until now, I hated going shopping.

We were like two school kids fooling around, riding on the back of the trolleys, playing hide and seek in the aisles. One day in Asda we were up to our normal antics when Jennie appeared with two cans of beans or something shaking and using them like maracas, an older couple were enthralled, wondering what was going on.

When we went to the checkout, he said loudly to his wife "Come on lets get in the queue behind this couple" (us), "they know how to enjoy themselves," We laughed and hugged each other knowing how fortunate we were to have that relationship.

We moved around the country several times with our jobs, it didn't matter where we were we had fun.

Holidays were always first class, we enjoyed a more than average lifestyle. One of our holidays to the states, New York to be exact, we got engaged.

To Have and To Hold

After buying the engagement ring from an exclusive jeweller on Fifth Avenue, we stayed at a hotel on Broadway and for seven days walked the Manhattan streets and central park. We took in and were intoxicated by the sights, sounds and different cultures of this vibrant exciting city.

The weather was glorious and that enabled us to do most of our eating, sitting outside of the many varied types, of restaurants, enjoying all the experiences.

Then off to Disney by internal flight, to see the theme parks and finally to the gulf coast to bask in the sun, on unspoiled, white sand beaches and walking out into the crystal clear blue water, with the fish swimming lazily around our legs, being dive-bombed by the numerous pelicans as they sought their meals.

Finishing the day off in luxurious restaurants with a quality of care and service, that in this country, sadly, is mostly only a dream. But all too soon it was time to go home, promising each other that one-day, we would come back and buy a property to rent out and live in.

Unfortunately that was never to be, when we got back world war three broke out, in our lives at home, at work and every other area of our lives.

Chapter 29

A Question of Faith

Penny and I were having the time of our lives on the face of it but underneath there was an undercurrent. As we had grown closer together we had started to talk more about the apparent difference between the faith which she had been brought up with and the things which I still believed in.

Her faith which she had not practiced for more than fifteen years now became the source of all our conversations. She had been schooled in the beliefs of the a well known sect.

Although for much of the same time I had not really done anything concerning my once concrete beliefs, when I was put to the test I couldn't deny the things that had happened in early life as told earlier in this book.

I found that when I was told that my own beliefs and faith were not correct, it caused me to do a real reassessment of the bible and the more I searched, the more convinced I became.

Although I had broken all the rules of conduct for my life, suddenly I was being questioned and taunted about the things I believed. The general idea was that we both needed to be of one mind to go on any further.

Penny had been brought up in a well known sect and challenged me to have a talk with one of their elders which I agreed to; but as we discussed their beliefs I became aware of the immense differences between us.

People outside created a lot of strife in our relationship, and circumstances that were beyond our control began to change the equilibrium of our wonderful life. Petty jealousies and different belief systems and added to that, serious ill health and I will call them interlopers, invaded us.

So for the next eighteen months we lived in a life of constant pressure with threats from all around that would test us to the limit and eventually broke the cord between us, soon after we decided to part completely over the most bizarre circumstances.

Building your happiness on an unsteady foundation usually won't work!!

As I began to read I became even more convinced of what I read. I turned to prayer again and thus began the most incredible spiritual journey and awakening to life in the spirit.

Chapter 30

Phil's Surprise!

I had managed to get another job, working part-time in an out-of-town Home Decorating store, but it wasn't easy to reach by bus and was quite heavy work. I was then out of work from September until May of 1998. In June, I went on a "Training for Work" scheme for three months, with the implied offer of a job at the end of it, but this didn't materialise.

Phil was also out of work during part of the summer, so when a call for help with a Tent Mission in Long Eaton went out, Phil went along to offer his services. It was here that he met a young lady called Miriam.

Apparently, it went something like this….Miriam noticed Phil and was very interested. Phil (this was unusual) didn't notice Miriam until a couple of days later and on enquiring who she was, was told that she already had a boyfriend.

Later that evening, Miriam, having realised that this was Mr Right, had dumped her non-Christian boyfriend!

To Have and To Hold

She cornered Phil, saying "I hear that you've been asking about me?" "Er, yes, I was." spluttered Phil! Four or five days later they were talking marriage!

Phil and Miriam were officially engaged in November, and Phil took Miriam to Lincolnshire to spend the day with Mike. Phil had primed Miriam as to the state of his relationship (or lack of it) with his Dad, and how he felt Mike had let him down in the past. However, Phil and Miriam were in for a big surprise!

When Phil and Miriam arrived, they discovered that Mike had been restored to the Lord, and so they enjoyed a great time of fellowship as Mike told them how it had all come about.

"So, Dad, how did you come back to the Lord?" Phil asked, excitedly.

"Well, about a week ago, I was driving in the car, when I suddenly found myself speaking in tongues! Strange, I thought! I haven't done that for years. Then I began to think about the peace and joy I had known when I was a Christian. But, I've got everything I could ever want, haven't I? As I pondered this, I realised that I was living in sin, "But, Lord, I really love Penny, I just can't give her up. If that's what you want, Lord, you'll have to do it, because I can't."

I was on my way to an appointment, and on entering the house I noticed a bible on the side. "Oh, a bible, you don't see those very often do you!" I said! "Oh!" he said, taking the bait I had given him, do you know much about the bible?"

"I'm a backslidden Christian," I went on, digging an even bigger hole for myself! I ended up telling him about what had happened in the car, and he asked if he could pray for me. I agreed and he prayed.

The next morning, at breakfast, Penny and I had an argument over something really stupid! I can't even remember what it was! She turned to me and said, "I want you out!" Now usually, I would have just laughed it off, but I just said "When?"

"By the end of the week" she replied.

"Ok, I said, thinking, "Wow, Lord, you don't hang about, do you?"

Well, it couldn't have happened at a worse time for me, I'd had a really good month, and I had just paid off all our debts, and now I've got nothing left. Penny found me a guest house, where I could stay, long term, so I've just moved out."

"Wow!" said Phil, "That's amazing!"

"Then I went into a garage, to fill up, and noticed a fish on the back of a car, I got chatting to the owner, and soon discovered that he is the Pastor of a local church!

He's invited me to go along, so everything is changing at the moment!"

Phil couldn't wait to tell me the news when he got home. "Mum," he said excitedly, "You'll never guess! Dad has come back to the Lord! We've just had a great time of fellowship with him!" Then Mike rang me and confirmed that yes, he had indeed got himself right with God.

On speaking to him I felt in my spirit that it was true, he really had been restored to grace. It was Sunday, so we went to the evening service at "T" Street, and the speaker was talking about desires.

He said, "We have been taught not to trust our own desires, because they will lead us astray. However, if you are walking with God in the ways of righteousness, then the desires of your heart are there because God put them there, and if God put them there, then He will fulfil them."

I sat there with a pounding heart, on the edge of my seat. At the end of the service, Malcolm, one of the Pastors, invited anyone who wanted someone to agree in prayer with them, for their desire, to come forward. I was the first on my feet, and practically ran to the front. I said, "Malcolm, my ex-husband of 16 years has been restored to the Lord. Will you agree in prayer with me for the restoration of my marriage?" Now, any self respecting Pastor would have taken me aside and recommended some counselling at the very least!! But Malcolm simply came into agreement with me, and from that point on, I KNEW that we would eventually get back together!

"First the blade, then the ear, after that the full corn in the ear!"

This was now the season of the ear of wheat. It was starting to look like what I had prayed for.

Now I needed to:
1. Water it with prayer.
2. Fertilize it with the Word.
3. Protect it from those who would uproot it.

At this time, I was working as a bus escort, taking disabled students to college. During Half Term in October, I was invited to go to a Hugh Christie School reunion, our first in 30 years! Many of my old school friends had kept in touch with each other, as they had stayed in the same area, but I had lost touch with everyone! It was great to see so many familiar faces, and the names that had become ingrained in my memory through the calling of the Register each morning, sprung to mind as we enthusiastically greeted each other! I stayed overnight with Mrs Collier, our neighbour, who still lives in the house opposite the one where I grew up.

The next day, I got the train to Canterbury, to visit my parents. Dad had been ill for some time with Prostate Cancer. I hadn't realised just how ill he was and now he looked very shrunken and hunched over. Why didn't I believe what I was seeing? Was I in denial? I don't know.

Dad had always been there for me, and although our relationship was perhaps a little formal as dad was not a demonstrative person, yet I knew he loved me and he had always tried to fulfil the role of father to the best of his ability, both to me and also to my children. In November, I wrote to him, to thank him for everything he had done for me, to express my respect and admiration for him, and to tell him that I loved him.

I know that if I had tried to say them to him, he would have just brushed them off, probably through embarrassment. So, I am glad that I wrote to him when I did, and didn't put off the idea till later, as we so often do, as I may well have missed my opportunity.

Chapter 31

Mike's Journey Back

During the period I spent away from God, I was always aware that for some reason, God, my Father, had never given up on me! No matter what I had done, in spite of the fact that I had completely given up on all the things which He saw as important and gone off in a totally different direction,

My God still loved me!

I often refer to those times now as being on an extending leash.

I went along to the church in Louth stayed as a permanent boarder with the guesthouse. I began to find out who I was, as myself, with no one else's input. I found that I had a lot of time to really think about the things that mattered, and started to spend much time in reflection.

One of my favourite sayings that I heard and then put into place in my life at that time was: "If you keep on doing what you've always done, you'll keep on getting

To Have and To Hold

what you always got. If you want to change some things in your life, you've got to change some *things* in your life", and that was exactly what I started to do.

I started, in many ways, a pilgrimage to search out the reasons why, even though I had immense success at everything I set out to do, it didn't last, whether in family or personal relationships, in finance or at work. It seemed that the more I tried, the worse it got.

Something had to change and in 1998 I went to a mid week house church and during the evening we were asked if anyone required prayer, I said 'Yes.'

One of the men who were leading the meeting put his hands on my head and began to pray, as he did, warmth started to flow through my hands and arms, at that His wife walked behind me and put her hands on the base of my spine and said "Heal him, Lord."

I had never met this couple before and what they didn't know was that since 1986, I had suffered with two split discs, at the base of my spine, which caused great pain and Sciatica which caused numbness, down to the toes of my right leg.

As they prayed, I started to fall backwards; I lay for quite some time with a great peace all over and a warm glow throughout my body. When I stood up there was no pain and I could easily bend to touch my toes, no pain and no effort.

For the next two years, I enjoyed growing in faith, belief and trust as God revealed himself to me in an even greater way. I became hungry for more of God and really for the first time, surrendered my *whole* life to His will.

He became as real to me in daily life as any human being and I began to find out more about His purpose for my life.

One of the things that really humbled me was the way He spoke peace into me. I deserved nothing. I had turned my back on Him and deserted the wife and children that He had given me.

All that I had done became very real and I talked to Him often to say how repentant I was. One day I was reading the Bible when it was as though the words lit up and jumped out from the page, "I have forgiven your sin and will remember it no more."

I couldn't forgive myself for the things from my past, never mind forget them! What an amazing God! I just sank to my knees and called out my praise to a loving caring God.

Chapter 32

The Year of 1999

The year of 1999 was one of highs and lows and at times very difficult, for all involved. It all started with such promise.

On New Year's Day, 1999, Mike arrived at the house and took us all out for a meal at a Chinese restaurant. Later, he explained to us, that he was really sorry for everything that had happened. However, it was in the past, and he couldn't do anything about it, except to draw a line beneath it and move on. Could we forgive him? Phil had phoned from Poland, whilst on a Mission trip, in the summer, to forgive his Dad. I told him that I had forgiven him years ago when it all took place.

Four days later, I had a phone call from my Mum, saying the Dad had died. Sarah and I went down to support my mum, staying until the funeral 10 days later.

Mike and Celia Deakin

Dad had been happy to have retired back to Canterbury, his home town. He had linked up with an old school chum and had become Honoury Chaplain, to many of the Ex-Serviceman's' Clubs in and around Canterbury. On the day of the Funeral, they all turned out in force!

Phil and Miriam arrived from Nottingham, to join us. We were surprised to find there were about 20 Standard Bearers, flanking the door of the church, which was packed, with standing room only!

I had not gone back to my job after New Year, but soon managed to get a job working in a Dry Cleaners pressing clothes. This only lasted till Easter. I signed up with an agency, and was offered a job as a filing clerk with a local firm, who later took me on as an Order Processor.

Meanwhile, Phil and Miriam had decided to get married in July and were trying to arrange the wedding, despite the fact that her dad, (also Phil) was suffering from stomach cancer and was sinking fast and died just after Easter.

The wedding went off very well, a happy occasion, but tinged with sadness, especially for Miriam's mum, who bravely gave her away. Mike and I seemed to have magnets attached to each other, and spent the day together.

To Have and To Hold

About three weeks later, Mike came over to see me one evening. We sat and chatted for quite a while, and then he asked if we could pray together, before he left. I agreed, and we prayed for the family and for each other. Afterwards, he said, "Thank you, I really felt a sense of unity with you, and for the first time, the children became OUR children, instead of your children or my children!"

Then, one Saturday in September, I was just walking into the kitchen, when I felt some words come to my mind, and I began to speak them out. ***"Blessed is she who believed, for there will be a fulfilment of those things which the Lord has spoken to thee of."***

I was surprised, because I was not used to receiving words of prophesy, and I had not been thinking about the promise. It just came "out of the blue" as they say! I checked and found it to be the words the angel Gabriel said to Mary in Luke Ch 1v45.

I thanked the Lord for His word to me, but didn't realise its full significance till Monday evening, when Mike rang me. He said, "Look, you are a very good friend, and you probably know me better than anyone else, but, I want it to stay as just a friendship, nothing more, is that alright?"

"Why, yyes!" I gulped, as he went on to explain that he didn't want to hurt me, but he didn't want me to get the wrong idea. He was engaged to Penny, and he wanted to marry her. Would I pray for her to become a Christian?

Well, I said "Yes, " but inside I was saying, "Ok, I will agree to be good friends, **but you don't know what I know!!!!" The word which the Lord gave me was to sustain me through the next two years!**

In November, Mike phoned to tell me that he felt something was wrong. He had been Top Salesman in his company, selling 1:2 or 1:3 appointments, suddenly, his sales had dropped to 1:9 and even that one had cancelled! Would I pray to see if there was some sin in his life that could have caused God to lift His favour from him? I said that I would.

The answer I got, was from Isaiah Ch 52: vs 11&12

"Depart! Depart! Go out from there, touch no unclean thing, go out from the midst of her; be clean, you who bear the vessels of the Lord. For you shall not go out with haste, nor go by flight, for the Lord will go before you, and the God of Israel will be your rear guard.

I believed God was saying that he should not be unequally yoked with an unbeliever and needed to break off his engagement. I was sure that was not what he wanted to hear! He didn't, for he took it to mean that he should leave his job and trust God to provide another means of income.

My sales didn't improve, and I could no longer afford to pay my board or for the Hire car which I used. John gave me £100.00 as seed to sow into my life and future ministry, which I used to buy a car! Friends from the church offered me the use of the summer house in which to sleep!

So, there I was driving to my new "luxury" accommodation, in an old "banger" of a car, when Satan started whispering in my ear. "Well just look at you! Is this where trusting in God gets you? Driving an old wreck and forced to sleep in someone's summer house in November and not even 10 pence to put in the phone box! Huh! Not a very clever decision, was it?

I was beginning to take on board the lies that were being poured in my ear, but then suddenly, the Holy Spirit began to show me his deceit. I now began under a fresh anointing to take authority and to withstand his affront!

"Satan!" I screamed! "Your lies show you up for who you are! You can say what you like, it doesn't bother me! My car is my own, bought and paid for, and I'm going to live with people who love and care for me, so I rebuke you in the name of Jesus!"

When I arrived at my friends' house, they expected me to be feeling somewhat defeated and deflated, having had to give up everything I had. Instead, I was really pumped up and greeted them heartily!

Celia ended the year by writing in her annual Christmas letter:

"Unto Him who is able to do exceedingly, abundantly above ALL that we ASK or Imagine, according to the power that works in us, unto Him be glory in the Church by Christ Jesus throughout all ages. Amen." Ephesians Ch3: vs 20, 21

Chapter 33

Catching the Fire!

I was still staying in the summer house with the family from our church, whose mom, Evelyn became my prayer partner and mentor.

She is a gracious lady with a keen sense of fun with a capital "F"! She just bounds about like a twenty-five year old. She is known by all the kids at church as Nan and is an example to all, of love personified.

During the time I have known Evelyn, our lives were knit together in the most amazing way and there are so many different stories of answered prayer that it would take another book to write them. Suffice it to say that I felt totally trusting and trusted by this wonderful lady.

One night, I was lying in bed, ready to go to sleep, when I thought of a book that I had purchased from the Bible bookshop. It was called 'Anointed or Annoying' and I lazily started to look at the first few pages.

It was talking of experiences of a pastor, who had got a fresh anointing from God and the difference in his life and the lives of his congregation. The way it was written was both amusing and challenging once I started reading, I could not put it down.

So, at about 3 o'clock in the morning, I finished reading it. I had the certain knowledge that whatever it was that had changed this man was what I needed in *my* life, and I had to follow up and speak to him. I tried to go to sleep, but there was something that had excited me about the book which had drawn out a hunger in me to know more of this move of God and the people of whom it spoke, so sleep did not come easily.

At breakfast, I told Evelyn of what I had read and my plan to try and contact them. I found out where the church was and obtained the phone number. They told me of a meeting which they suggested I should go to, at Stockton on Tees, at a small place called Yarm. All of my questions would be answered by attending that meeting.

Little did I know by how much! Just from reading the book, I knew, there was no question as to *if* I would be going to the meeting! So, Evelyn and I started to plan our journey. As the time drew nearer, there was a real sense of expectancy, we were sure that something very significant was going to come from this journey!

To Have and To Hold

When we arrived, the spectacular entrance hall and auditorium was the exact replica of a vision, which Evelyn had described to me some two weeks before.

There was a real sense of the presence of God that seemed to linger over the foyer. That feeling never left or decreased in the two & half days that we were there, a sense of being on Holy Ground.

On the Thursday, after preliminaries, all the pastors and leaders were called to the front and again there was this sense of the closeness of God. Evelyn and I spoke out, that this time was a time of life changing and destiny.

As the evening continued, the leaders came back into the congregation and prayed for the rest of us. As they did, a feeling of true unity came upon the congregation, of something like a thousand people that were assembled.

After this we went to our accommodation. Friday morning we were up and away early, to join the prayer meeting that was taking place. When we arrived the awesome presence of God pervaded the place and we knew this was going to be significant.

As the day unfolded, many things were happening supernaturally, as people came and met with our Lord Jesus Christ. The story of Bartimaeus was read out and it was explained, the pastor said that this cry of

Bartimaeus was the cry that stopped God and if we likewise would find that cry, as Bartimaeus was healed, so would we.

For me this was a most pertinent time, as I faced the hurt from my childhood. I let go of the hurt and anger that had been lying inside, for more than forty years. I had no awareness of this situation until now. All I knew was that as I cried out to God, all the hurt was taken away.

I felt that God took me by my coat collar and lifted me up. "Mike," He said, "when you were 17 or 18, you had an excuse for blaming everything on your upbringing, but you're a man now, so it's time to take responsibility for your own actions. If you will confess your un-forgiveness, I will change your life, take away the bitter roots and set your heart on fire for Me."

I don't want you to think that all of this was easy, because forty years of hatred is a lot to get rid of! During the next couple of hours, my emotions swung like a pendulum inside, I went into abject misery, to total elation, then back again and back again, until there was no hurt left, no more tears to cry.

When I stood up, I felt there was a freshness, and a clearness that I had been longing for and a peace within. Electricity was coursing through my body, which I now know as the power of the Holy Spirit. On the Saturday,

To Have and To Hold

after many more times of wonderful fellowship, we left for home, thrilled at what had happened and knowing that we would never be the same again.

On the way home, we met up with my son Philip, who was totally awestruck with all the things that had happened and were still happening. We were singing, praying and praising, so much so, that we had to stop the car on three occasions, because the presence of God was so evident in the car, what a momentous journey that was!

When we arrived home there was so much happening that it's difficult to know where to begin! The power of God that was inside us, meant that we saw many miracles of healing, large and small. People who had phobias, fears and addictions, were set free when we prayed as individuals or together.

I was now employed selling door to door, for a company who supplied gas and electricity, but when I returned from Yarm, I started to move in a completely new dimension, in the Anointing of The Holy Spirit.

As I was walking down the street, I found myself wanting to pray. I began speaking in tongues and it seemed as though I could hear Holy Spirit giving me guidance as to which particular door or house to go to. When I did as I was directed, I had very unusual meetings with the occupants, and I was often being asked in, with no introduction.

Inside, I found people with particular health problems or dilemmas of every sort imaginable and found that after praying for them the problem was no more.

I started phoning Celia, to ask her to pray for different people and situations that I was coming across every day, *little did I realise what the Lord was doing!*

There are probably those that will read this book and think or say these things can't happen. All I can say is they do and they did, it's as simple as trusting God to do what needs to be done. There's nothing special about me, what you've read so far proves that, but there's something special about our amazing God. Who is the same yesterday, today and forever!

This proved to be the start, of some of the most inspiring, thrilling and blessed times of my life. Wherever I went the Spirit of God did wonderful things, healing bodies, and setting lives free, all to the glory of God!!!

This life in God is available to all through the death and resurrection of Jesus Christ His son.

When I started to write this book, I wasn't sure where it would take me.

As British people we are told from a very young age, don't to let people see the inner us, it makes you vulnerable, more than once I have been told that my transparency makes people feel uncomfortable, because they are challenged by it.

I now know, that it is the only way, to real peace, so if Jesus says I'm okay, then why should I worry about acceptance from anyone else?

What happened was that I became passionate about people. I believe that inside every person there is a seed of greatness. My mission in life is to help each person, no matter what colour, creed, background, childhood, or environment they came from, to reach their full potential! By living the life I now live, I can help others to succeed and grow.

Chapter 34

Spreading the Fire

During the next ten months, my life became one of total fulfilment, with a sense of destiny driving me forward, but in ways that seemed as natural as breathing.

The most obvious thing that had changed, was that along with the sense of purpose, went such a tranquillity and peace, that I never seemed to be in a rush to go anywhere, or do anything and yet seemed to achieve more each day.

The year 2000 continued at this pace into June, when Evelyn and I attended the Christ for all Nations Fire Conference, in Birmingham, where we were privileged to take the role of counsellors in a congregation of around eight thousand people.

This was quite an experience, where we saw physical healings of cancers and one case in particular, where a lame seventy-four year old was healed and proved it by

To Have and To Hold

throwing away the frame he had been using and did a run around the arena to give the glory to God.

From there on, the year continued to move at a fast pace. At work, my boss had spoken to me about becoming a Roving Manager. Touring the country to encourage and be a stand in for those sick or on holiday, this is where the coincidences of my life were about to gather momentum again.

In early August, I phoned my Mom in Birmingham. Our relationship had not been good, to say the least, so I had rung more from a sense of duty, than anything else. Something she said made me phone her back and I told her I was going to visit her.

When I had been at the Fire Conference, I met a man named Bob. We got on very well and he invited me to visit him when I next came to Birmingham.

I had said the chances were remote but thanks for the invite. Everyone who really knew me was aware that Birmingham was the last place I wanted to go; I had hated the place with a passion all my life. However, only two months later, I called Bob to arrange the visit!

When I went to see Mom, I prayed all the way, as I knew that there were a lot of problems that needed to be sorted out. My mother had been suffering with Parkinson's disease for many years. She also had other problems which were associated with her alcoholism.

Mike and Celia Deakin

When I arrived, we sat and did all the niceties, two of my siblings were also there but left after about forty five minutes, so now I could deal with the real reason for my visit.

I pulled the footstool over in front of Moms' chair and took hold of her hands and said "Mom, will you forgive me for my lack of love, my un-forgiveness and hatred that I have held towards you all my life?"

She replied, "It's me that needs forgiveness, for the way I treated you."

I said, "I already forgave you, will you forgive me?"

She said, "Yes." and for the first time since I can remember Mom and I cuddled like Mother and Son, no longer like acquaintances and distant ones at that!

Later that day, I went to stay at Bob's and spent the weekend with them, at a Caribbean festival around several churches.

On Monday, I was leaving the church for home and saw two guys outside a block of flats in one of the less well off areas of Birmingham. I found myself praying for them and the area.

I remember talking to Jesus and saying, "That it felt as though this area was drawing me." and then trying to argue with Him that I didn't want anything to do with any part of Birmingham. But then instantly I knew that I would give Him anything He asked of me.

On Monday evening, I went to Grapevine, a tent crusade in Lincoln, where I met some men from an organization called Betel of Britain. Betel help people off the street, who were drug addicts or with alcohol abuse problems.

They take people without any cost to them and all they ask is that there is a commitment of one year to the program.

The results of the program are nothing short of miraculous! It is quite usual for people with heroin addiction to come off their addiction within two or three weeks. The thing that takes the time is getting to the root of the problem and dealing with the cause of the addiction.

So very often, it can take many months or even years, to deal with the underlying problem. However, if they find faith in Jesus the whole transformation can happen almost overnight!

The real miracle of Betel goes from strength to strength, because you have ex-addicts talking with addicts with real belief and zeal, due to the change that they have known in their own lives.

Later that same day, my boss Steve called, to discuss the new position as a Roving Manager. He started by saying, "I know you're not going to like what I'm about to ask you to do, but in this case I desperately need your help."

"What do you mean?" I said.

"I want you to take over someone's team while they're on holiday; it's only for two weeks."

"Where's that? I asked.

"Birmingham." he said.

"When?" I queried.

"On Friday this week!"

"Ok!" I say.

The phone went silent and I asked if he was still there, "Yes!" he said, "but I expected a long drawn out discussion and argument."

"Long story Steve! No discussion! No argument, just give me the details please."

I knew that somehow, not only was I going to succeed in my job in Birmingham but also, that this was going to be a special time in so many ways, although I didn't know how.

I went to see my pastor at the church and discussed what was happening. He confirmed many of my thoughts and said he believed that this was not just a two-week move. The result of the meeting was that John (My Pastor) suggested that I should discuss My plans with the senior Pastor, this I did.

At the meeting Lee said that He agreed with what John had said and after a short meeting suggested that we should have a time of prayer together, during which he said that there was no specific clear leading that he could give me. However, he had some verses that he felt I would find relevant, although he was not sure that I would like what he was about to say.

I agreed that we should continue and look at the verses. They were:

"This is the second thing you do, you cover the altar of the Lord with tears, with weeping and crying: so he does not regard the offering any more, nor receive it with goodwill from your hands.

Yet you say, for what reason? Because the Lord has been witness between you and the wife of your youth, with whom you have dealt treacherously: yet she is your companion and your wife by covenant.

But did He not make them one having a remnant of the Spirit? And why one? He seeks godly offspring. And let none deal treacherously with the wife of his youth.

For the Lord God of Israel says that He hates divorce, for it covers ones garments with violence, says the Lord of Hosts. Therefore take heed to your spirit that you do not deal treacherously."

Malachi ch2 verses 13:16

Mike and Celia Deakin

These had become familiar to me since this was the third time that they had been prophesied or read over me but I was reluctant to receive them.

So off I went to spend two weeks with Bob, this turned out to be five weeks, not two, but in that time I was cared for like a son by Bob and his family.

After five weeks, I went into a friends' caravan, out at a place called the Clent Hills. What a beautiful spot it was, totally secluded up in the hills looking out into a wooded glade.

This was the ideal time to spend time in meditation, reflection and prayer. I took the opportunity gratefully and felt that this was a time of inward growth.

I have found that as I spend time listening to God, He never disappoints me, He always shows up! The time seemed to fly by and autumn turned to winter. The winds increased and the caravan was tossed about like a kite in the wind, so the time to look for a more permanent home became evident.

Chapter 35

Y2000

The New Millenium may have started with a bang for the rest of the world, but for me it was a bit of a damp squib! In January, I started yet another new job this time doing telesales until May and then temping as a filing clerk for a couple of weeks.

Mum came up to stay with me at Easter, and we enjoyed some time together, going to Derbyshire for the day and shopping in town. My friend Judith invited us to join her at a Passover meal, which a church near her was holding.

Mum was unhappy in Canterbury, and feeling rather lonely. I tried to persuade her to move up to Nottingham, to be near us. On her return home, she said Nottingham was too busy and noisy for her, and she had decided to stay where she was. The very next day, she received a list of available properties for retired clergy, one of which was 2 minutes from her brother's house in Sussex. She went to look at it, and loved it! She was moved in within 3 weeks! God had moved on her behalf, and she knew it!

In April, God gave me a prophesy, which I brought to the church: *"Is the arm of the Lord shortened? Is anything too hard for the Lord? Is anything too hard for the Lord? If you ask anything in my name and according to my will, it SHALL be done for you, so believe and receive!"*

About a week later, the Word for Today exhorted us to:

"Allocate and lay claim to the "Promised Land"! We are not to live in limitation! Possess what God has promised. Caleb, at 85 years old, was still going strong and took on the Giants in order to possess his promises. It is not beyond you!"

So, I began writing out various promises which the Lord had given me down through the years and laying claim to them. I found that "The Word for Today" was like a personal letter to me from God, it was so relevant to my everyday situations and became a "must read"!

In July, I was approached by the Director of our churches charitable arm, with a view to taking over as Manageress of the local Charity Shop. He asked me to pray about it and to let him know my decision. I knew in my heart that this was just what I was seeking, so I accepted eagerly! After a couple of half days, to learn the ropes, I was on my own!

I just loved it! I was in effect my own boss, I could arrange the goods the way I wanted, and soon got it looking attractive. Trade seemed to be picking up and many people became regular shoppers (or at least "browsers")! I got to know many people in the area and sometimes had opportunities to share the gospel with them in non-threatening ways.

Our shop was also very blessed by the fact that a member of our church had a business selling hand built Three Piece Suites. As part of their selling technique, they offered the customers a discount on their old suite. Most people were happy to have someone take it away, so to get a discount was an extra plus. All these suites were given to our charity. Some had to be taken to the tip, but the good ones could be sold, as long as they had a fire proof label. I had to learn how set a price, and also how to haggle the price with potential customers!

God was continuing to encourage me, and I wrote many of them in my journal, such as the following:

On October 27th "The Word for Today" said, *"Yet amid all these things, we are more than conquerors!" Rom Ch 8: v 37.*

You are more than a conqueror when:

1. *You have a sense of victory before the battle even begins.*

2. *You know you have the solution before the problem even arises.*
3. *You're confident that you have God's approval – regardless of whose rejection you may be feeling.*

Sometimes, it's the LENGTH not the strength of the trial that shakes us up.

If so, listen:

"Do not throw away your confidence. You need to persevere, so that when you have done the will of God, you will receive what He has promised!"

Heb Ch 10 vs 35, 36.

In my annual Christmas letter, I wrote:

"Mike and I have become good friends and are in regular contact by phone….he has involved himself in an organisation called Betel (which) seeks to rehabilitate drug addicts and introduce them to Jesus. He is really going on with God and is allowing God to heal all the broken areas of his life. It is taking time but that is just an indication of how much he has changed, as the old, impetuous Mike would have rushed in to do it his way!"

On: December 24th "TWFT" said:

"Handling Rejection. *"Consider Him who endured such opposition….so that you will not grow weary and loose heart." Heb Ch12: 3"*

To Have and To Hold

December 29th 2000 The Word for Today read, The Law of Progression

"First the blade, then the ear, after that the full corn in the ear!" Mark 4:28

1. The "I don't know" Season

Your seed is in the ground but you're in the dark, the how and when is up to God....all you know is that IT WILL!

2. "The Blade Season"

A tiny blade of encouragement that the answer is on its way.

3. "The Ear Season"

It starts to look like what you prayed for

    a. Water it with prayer

    b. Fertilize it with the word

    c. Protect it from those who would uproot it

4. "The full corn season"

When you hear the words "Put in the sickle, because the harvest is come!"

Recognise it....Reach for it....Receive it! Stand fast and keep trusting! Your harvest and answer are on its way!

The full corn season was just beginning!

Chapter 36

The Waiting Game

"The Word for Today" continued to speak powerfully into my situation.

My journal reads: *January 5th. Receiving from God.*

"Whoever shall say......and shall not doubt.....shall have whatever he saith." Mark Ch 11:v23

1. **Make up your mind.** *Be tenacious. Don't get comfortable without it. Pain leads to progress.*
2. **Visualise your victory.** *Challenge your Giants.*
3. **Speak to your situation.** *Line up what you say with God's Word.*

Make His opinion yours, His Word yours and the mountain WILL become your servant!

I believed that the Full Corn Season was upon me. But there were still a few hurdles to clear! Not least of which was patience. What? More patience? Yes, *and* dying to my own desires.

January 19th "TWFT"
The Danger of Impatience.

"Other seed fell on shallow soil." Mark Ch 4 vs 5,6.

Ask God to keep you in His perfect timing – not one step ahead nor one step behind.

When is my due season? Gal Ch 6: v9.

It's when:

1. God knows you're ready.
2. When everyone else involved is ready
3. And when it fits into His overall plan.

*The trouble is that we don't hang around long enough to see the finish of great things, because they take **time**. If it's thrown together too quickly, it's not likely to last because **character is built during hard times of waiting.** Without that, you'll have no root system and you'll wither because you can't handle the pressure.*

When you learn to respect and appreciate the times of waiting, then God will go to work in earnest in your life. ***Even though you can't see what's happening, the thing that will bring you the most fulfilment is happening NOW – behind the scenes!"***

And it was!!

February 11th "TWFT" said: *"My times are in Thy Hand" Ps 31v15 In God's Waiting Room*

Understanding God's timing enables me to co-operate with His plan for my life. When you don't know, learn to wait with confidence on the One who does! If you're going to walk with Him and enjoy it, start letting God be God! Don't attempt to take the lead role in your relationship with Him – He has that role…and He won't give it to us! He gives the instructions and we follow – even though we may not <u>like</u> or <u>understand</u> the way He takes us!

Timing is an important issue here. Why does God take sooo long to do things? ***Because trust requires unanswered questions****, that keeps your faith growing!*

God has a plan and a time, so while He's getting us ready, He keeps us – in His waiting room! Is that where you are today? (Here I answered with a big **YES!**) – ***It's only as you reach new levels of maturity, that he releases new levels of blessing into your life!***

In my journal I wrote: "Today I pray, Lord, I know you love me and that your plan and your timing are perfect, so I rejoice and trust in you. Amen."

However, that didn't stop me from sending a "Fun" Valentines card! Had I really been paying attention as in "not taking the lead role"? Mike didn't acknowledge the card, but then it was anonymous!

To Have and To Hold

A month later, Mike phoned me to ask if he could come over to talk to me about something really important! That evening, Mike made it quite clear that he did not see us as anything more than very good friends. He wanted no deeper relationship with me than that.

"TWFT" for that day, March 13th read as follows:
When doors are closed

"See I have place an open door before you that no-one can shut!" Rev Ch 3: v8

"The one person I "knew" would fulfil all my dreams has walked away. Slam! Slam! Slam! Doors I thought God had opened, have become curtains of steel! Despite my disappointment, I will remember that ***"God is STILL directing my steps!*** *Ps 37 v23.*

The path I am now on will bring Him the ultimate glory and me the ultimate benefit.

I may protest that "There's nobody else I want! From my limited perspective, that may be true – but God alone can see into the future."

Somehow, God gave me peace about it all. I had been to see Malcolm, just a week before to ask his advice, as I was confused as to Mike's intentions. He said I had a choice, to ask him, or wait for him to tell me. He assured me that I was still very marriageable, which cheered me up no end! I decided to wait, and Mike had given me a clear answer.

So, for now, I would just carry on as before, working in the shop and trusting my future to the Lord. Phil and Miriam had announced at Christmas, that they were expecting their first child. The baby was due in August. I had booked a holiday in Italy with Oak Hall again; I really hoped the baby didn't decide to arrive early! So I had plenty to occupy my mind!

One day, Tony, who supplied the three piece suites, came to my shop to give his business perspective on how we ran the store. I had not met him before, but Phil had and had told me that Mike used to work for him, for a Home Improvement company.

During his visit, I mentioned that I was Mike's ex-wife. Suddenly, I had his full attention! He was interested to hear from him, would I give him his business card. I agreed to do this, so, some time later, Mike contacted him and they arranged to meet up.

Tony was keen to get Mike to work for him, knowing that he was one of the top salesmen in the country! Mike accepted his offer and began work the following week, selling top class hand made upholstery and enjoyed the challenge of selling in customers homes and at the local studios.

Chapter 37

Mike Settles in Birmingham

In November of 2000, as I had done for the last few years; I went into rental property, a three-bed detached house with a good-sized garden and all was going well.

It had turned out that the best help I could be was to help the people of Betel with driving lessons. Since where I lived near where Betel was, it made sense to attend their church.

I made many firm friends and enjoyed fellowship with the guys and girls and also had the privilege to make real friends with several of the leaders. These friendships have lasted over the last six years in spite of time and distance.

From the beginning of 2000, I had spent a lot of time on the phone to Celia, my ex wife, sharing what was happening in our lives. During these phone calls we were able to talk about what had happened to cause the break-up of our marriage, settling numerous misunderstandings that we both had.

I had been to Nottingham, where she and the children lived, on several occasions and we felt easy with each other, but then Celia seemed to start looking for more than a friendship and I pulled away like a scalded cat.

I even went to the trouble one night, to drive up and clarify the situation, saying, "We shall never get back together, if you want more than friendship lets call it a day. You're probably the best friend I have ever had, but that's as far as it goes."

This was about March of 2001, and probably due to my own misgivings and long work hours, our contact slowed down somewhat.

Penny and I were still in contact. I knew that I could never agree to the doctrines of her faith but she tried every way possible to get me to have more talks with their elders.

She gave me all sorts of literature to read including an interlinear bible and concordance, the idea was that I should read their literature without any recourse to my own bible. This I agreed to but the more I read the more the Holy Spirit brought to my remembrance all the verses I had learned in my early days as a Christian.

All that was happening was that my head was going into turmoil, the more I read the more confused I became, on the one hand I really loved Penny and wanted to be with her, on the other I became more and more convinced that what I was reading did not match up to what I believed and since in this matter there could be no compromise there could never be a future.

Chapter 38

The Post Dated Promise

During this time I knew Mike was going through a difficult time. He had lost his Mum, Phil and Sarah had gone down for the funeral, but Mike didn't want me to go. I didn't think he was that close to his mother, so I thought he would cope alright.

I was concerned about his confusion over literature given him by a well known Sect. It seemed that Penny wanted him to embrace *her* faith, so that they could marry. I told him "It's Satan who is the author of confusion, so if you feel confused, guess where it's coming from!"

I shared my concerns with my friend, Judith and we both prayed that God would bring him clarity of mind. I had also shared with her and others that I believed Mike and I would get back together.

I believe that you need to keep confessing those things you desire from God. I also believe in visualising it coming to pass. I'd always been a daydreamer anyway, so that came to me quite naturally. But when God gives you a dream, you need to be able to "see it" before you see it!

At the end of July, I went on holiday to Italy! I had a fantastic time visiting Pisa, Florence and the Isle of Elba. I shared a tent with a young girl named Mireille.

One night, laying in our sleeping bags in the dark, we started chatting. In the course of our conversation, I shared my story with her. To my surprise, (she wasn't a Christian, then) she began to pray for us, I was very touched by her prayer, and KNEW that God had heard her prayer. Later, when I tried to contact her to let her know that God had answered her prayer, I was unable to reach her.

August 1st "TWFT"
"POST DATED PROMISES."
"Though it lingers, wait for it; it will certainly come!" Hab Ch 2:vs 2,3.

"God works on both ends of the line and prepares you for 'it' (whatever that may be). Visionaries are impatient – the greater the vision, the harder to wait! But it's an essential part of the process.

Have you been asking "Lord, how long will my passion be there, but my place be here? How long do I have to keep this promise in my heart?

WAIT! Your appointment is still on God's calendar! Listen! "There's never been the slightest doubt in my mind, that the God who started this great work in you, would keep at it and bring it to a flourishing finish!"

Phil Ch1: v 6 TM

Even though your promise may be post-dated, remember whose signature is on the cheque!"

I arrived home to discover that there had been a change of policy in the Charity I worked for, which necessitated them giving me a months notice. I was terribly upset and hurt at the way it had been done. I phoned Mike to tell him the news and to ask him to pray.

On Saturday, August 11th I had a call at the shop from Phil, to announce the safe arrival of our new baby granddaughter, Grace. The shop was usually very quiet on Saturday afternoons, so I arranged to close early, and go over to see them at the hospital.

The phone rang again, it was Mike. "Have you heard the news?"

"Yes! Isn't it great? Congratulations, Granddad!"

"Will you get a card for them, from both of us?" Mike asked. Before I had a chance to marvel at such a request, he added, "What are you doing tomorrow?"

"Nothing special, why?"

"Would you like to come down to Birmingham, to see where I live? We can have a meal together," he suggested.

"That would be lovely", I replied.

"I've got to work in the morning," he said.

"That's ok, I can go to the station straight from the church." So it was arranged.

I shut the shop, met Sarah and we went over to see the new addition to the family, picking up my camera and a card on the way. Mother and baby were doing fine, Miriam looked as fresh as a daisy! She certainly didn't look as though she'd given birth just six hours previously!

Back home I walked around the house and garden – aware that I would soon be moving from this house. I was about to reap the harvest for which I had waited so long!

Chapter 39

Put in the Sickle, it's Harvest Time!

At the beginning of August I had really started searching and praying about my future in Gods' kingdom. One morning I got up and felt a compulsion to put one of my Bible teaching videos on. I had owned it for some time, but never seen it. As I was watching it, I felt as though I was drifting in and out of a vision. The only thing that I got from it was the words, "The power of life and death is in the tongue."

In my mind I was drawing up a list of things in my life. The areas of responsibility and interest, things like work, Betel, church, ministry, home and family. Suddenly, Celia's name was written all across everything else in my mind. That was a real surprise! Not knowing what else to do, I argued with myself and tried to erase it, but it kept coming back! So, I started to pray to find out what it all meant.

I had a sense that I should contact Celia and invite her down to Birmingham for Sunday lunch. I reasoned that since she had recently lost her job and none was forthcoming in Nottingham, maybe she would have more success in Birmingham.

In prayer I laid out three fleeces, as tests, to check out my thoughts. Firstly, would she agree to the visit on a Sunday, (this was normally a very busy day for her). Secondly, if she found work, she would have to sell up and I knew that she saw the house as being a large part of her security and thirdly, she would agree to move to Birmingham.

I decided not to phone until Saturday, because really, I was uneasy about all the implications of the fulfilment of my current thoughts. I was also working on Sunday, so I wouldn't be free until 1 o'clock.

Celia would only be coming for an afternoon visit, with all this in mind, I phoned her. Much to my surprise, of all the 52 weeks of the year, this weekend she was free. It was no problem to come in the afternoon, as it meant that she could attend church first, so the plans were set.

By Sunday, I was like a cat on a hot tin roof, feeling very uneasy and trying to think of a reason to cancel, but no logical one came to mind. So, off I went to work, the appointment was both local and successful, but the outcome made it that I was running late to collect Celia from the train station.

I rang and said I would be about an hour late, "No problem" she said, the train has been held up, so I gave in graciously and knew that I couldn't get out of the meeting.

Incidentally, I realized that there were an awful lot of those coincidences happening again! When I got near to New Street Station, I phoned her mobile, "I'm just getting off the train," she said. She came out onto the road and met me as I arrived, perfect timing or what?

We went home, collected a Chinese take-away and sat and talked, after which she went to bed and I stayed on the sofa to get ready for an early start the next day.

Next morning, I was up and out, to go on a driving lesson, with Betel. So, leaving Celia asleep I went off for my days work, knowing that Celia would catch the midday train. I tried to phone a couple of times in the afternoon, to make sure she had arrived safely, but could get no response due to a poor signal.

As I finished work my mobile rang, Celia was on the line, "Where are you?" I asked, 'At home,' she replied, realizing she was on her mobile the penny clicked that she was still at my home.

I asked why she hadn't caught the train and she told me it was her day off and she'd return the following day.

I went off home and found her cooking a steak meal, wasn't really sure how I felt about that, but the next thirty minutes sealed my destiny.

The short version of what happened is probably appropriate at this stage. While talking, I asked about her work and passed the questions concerning the other two fleeces spoken about earlier.

To the question about moving to be in Birmingham she replied that it wouldn't be her number one choice to live, but it would depend on the incentive to do it.

(This is where I show that I am a totally logical, thinking, in control, sane human being. "I wish").

"You mean like if I asked you to marry me"? What? I'm thinking! Where did that come from?

But the glint in her eyes showed that there was no misunderstanding of what had just been said!

(Now comes the death knell!)

"Well, do it properly then"! She says. So, like a lamb to the slaughter, down I go on one knee and seal my fate. "Will you marry me"?

No going back now, the final nail is in the coffin!

"She says yes".

The following day, off she goes knowing that we have agreed not to tell anyone else, at least until we settle the details of where and when. After the initial shock we both went to talk to long trusted friends and although they wanted to be excited, they were cautious with their response.

Celia and I were left to sit down and weigh up the pros and cons which means we virtually cut off contact and proceeded to back pedal at ninety miles an hour.

Celia especially, needed to consider at length, the implications of selling up and moving away from the friends who had stood by her, during the eighteen years we had been apart.

I was looking at the whole situation and I suppose feeling very guilty, because I knew that we were going to have to re-run all that happened, with people that had stayed loyal to Celia and not least of all the children themselves.

If I was truthful, I was conscious that I would be meeting all the people that I had let down, when I had walked out of our marriage and our friendships. There is always a price to pay, to repair the things we break, without thought of the consequences.

About three to four weeks on, we decided together to start moving forward again, but this time with a little more thought.

Firstly, we made an appointment with marriage councillors from Celia's church, then we booked the wedding service with the pastor.

We also went out to a quiet sea shore, in Lincolnshire, to clarify any issues that could cause problems.

By having an intense conversation that took up most of the day, we both knew, with out a shadow of doubt, that we were walking in the will of God by getting remarried, because He had never seen us as anything but man and wife.

Chapter 40

Gathering the Harvest in.

We got a mixed reception to our news; Phil was thrilled to bits, having prayed for his dad to come back since he was 6 years old! Sarah was not so enthralled at the prospect, but that could have been because it put her in a difficult position. I was moving to Birmingham and selling the house but she was still living at home. She didn't want to leave Nottingham, so was obliged to find suitable accommodation. The nestling was being pushed out of the nest and she was not yet ready to fly.

My friend, Sarah, came to talk to me as a good friend should, to ask some searching questions about how I saw the whole situation. She wanted to ascertain that I was not jumping into a situation I couldn't handle and that I had thought carefully about all the implications.

We also went to see Malcolm, whom we had asked to take the Service. He asked Mike, "Are you in love with Celia?"

Mike replied very honestly, "No, not 'in love' with all the bells and whistles! But I do love her, and I know in my heart that it is right for us to marry." Malcolm thanked him for his candid answer, and said, "I would have been far more concerned if you had said 'Yes', so, I am satisfied that it is right to go ahead. I already know how Celia feels, so I have no need to ask, do I?"

We celebrated Grace's first Christmas along with Mike's 50th Birthday! Then I got busy with some last minute decorating of the house in order to put it on the market.

I asked our daughter, Sarah to be my bridesmaid but she wasn't keen on doing it alone so I asked my friend Judith as well.

Mike asked Phil to be his Best Man and my mum agreed to give me away. However, mum later had second thoughts, so I asked Phil if he could double up in giving me away!

We chose dresses and Mike and Phil chose their outfits; we chose hymns and choruses and booked a venue. I typed up the Order of Service, and the Invitations, got them printed and sent out!

In between all this, we celebrated Sarah's 21st Birthday! She managed to find a little terraced house to rent, and moved in about ten days before the wedding.

Mike and Celia Deakin

We also did quite a lot of commuting between Nottingham and Birmingham. One weekend in February, I went down to Birmingham, so we could go house hunting. I prayed, "Lord, you know we only really have one day to find a house, please will you lead us to the house YOU want us to buy, because I don't want to go round a string of houses first!"

We had a look at one of the local papers, then we set out in the car, to an area near the Airport. We drove around for a bit, looking at houses in the paper from the outside, then went to find the two local Estate Agents offices. When we went into the second one, the girl said, "I've got this one, it's just come in, we haven't even typed up the details yet! We went to see it, and just knew within ten minutes of being there that this was the right one!

My house was sold and so I packed everything into boxes, but 19 years in one house means a lot of excess baggage! I moved out a week before the wedding and stayed at a friend's house, booking into a hotel with Judith for the night before the big day.

* * 🐝 * *

The time just seemed to fly by and suddenly we were a week away from the wedding day. We had a phone call from the venue we had booked for the reception, they were changing all the agreed features of the reception, no space for the disco, can't set up before 4pm, tables for food can't be laid until 4pm and to finish it off, only a maximum of seventy five guests could be accommodated.

Our estimate had been for a minimum of one hundred and twenty people, we actually ended up with one hundred and fifty people. Let's just look at the situation. One week before your wedding, the booking venue is no good, what would you do?

Well, what we did was pray and so we found ourselves led through all sorts of coincidences! This included the fact that our new venue, the only one we approached, had bookings for every Saturday before and after our 27th April wedding day for two years! The lady we dealt with said she had tried every way to book that date but with no success!

On the day, our son, Phil, forgot the wedding rings and had to go home to fetch them, about a 20 mile round trip!

Malcolm greeted me at the door and broke the news that Phil had just left to get the rings. The Service was due to start at 1.30 pm, in the centre of Nottingham. There is always a lot of traffic in the city, but lunch time on Saturdays was particularly busy.

We waited downstairs, in the foyer, whilst Mike and the congregation waited upstairs. As we stood there, so people kept on arriving, as they were not used to the one way system! So we came to the realisation that we were following God's timing not our own!

In all, thirty or more people, who were lost in and around Nottingham, managed to arrive in time to be involved in the whole service!

Eventually, just as Malcolm was saying that we may have to borrow some rings in order to go on with the service, Phil and Miriam arrived and I was able to walk down the isle on Phil's arm.

We made it at last!

The ceremony was a great success and everyone commented on both the service and the reception. What fantastic time, with all our friends and family from thirty years, all meeting together, and in many cases, for the first time.

This is what we wrote on the Order of Service:

Celebrate With Us!

For with Man, This is Impossible

BUT WITH GOD
ALL THINGS ARE POSSIBLE

We want to thank you all for coming and making a special day even more so by your being here!

We also want to thank all those who have faithfully prayed for us both down through the years.

You are today seeing the answer to those prayers! We trust that God will pour out such a blessing that you will not be able to contain it!

It really was a dream wedding in every way!

Even the photograph session was relaxed and fun, as we strolled around the grounds of Nottingham Castle posing for photos along the way!

Then we went to the reception, which again was very relaxed and enjoyable as we introduced friends to people they had heard us talk about for years but never met! It was wonderful!

After the reception, we drove to the hotel for the night, ready for our honeymoon in the Algarve, in Portugal.

It was good to really wind down and enjoy the rugged beauty of this delightful country. We had decided to travel on public transport, so that we could concentrate on the views around us and of course on each other.

During the time away, our solicitor and estate agent managed to mess up the completion of our property purchase even though we tried to deal with things by mobile.

It became increasingly obvious, that we would not be able to move into our own home on our return and my boss Martin, kindly came to the rescue, by inviting us to stay with him and his partner until completion, which finally happened on the 10th May 2002.

We moved in and began to build a new life together. We found a local church, who welcomed us and made us feel at home. I began to find my way around; there were so many shopping areas, it took me a while to decide which was most suitable!

After a happy ever after, fairy tale wedding, it was now that the 'rubber hit the road'! Here we were at last, my dream had come true! But now what? I had lived and prayed and longed for this time! Now I had everything I had ever wanted. But it was almost an anticlimax! You know, the Post Christmas, January feeling?

I found that now I had no goal in life, I had moved away from all my familiar surroundings. I had lost my home and I felt like a tree that had been uprooted and re-planted! After the harvest comes the winter and this was certainly a winter season in my life. Mike was often working long hours, so I had plenty of time to contemplate my situation!

Again I found myself thrown on God; it was a time for all the growing to be done in the dark, underground, unseen ready to burst forth in the spring sunshine. Don't get me wrong, I was happy and as our love grew we began re-discovering each other. After all we had been through; we were now two very different people to the two young things we were first time around!

I realised that just as when we had married the first time, so it was this time, in that I needed to put God first. He was the one who satisfied my needs, he gave the joy and peace, strength and hope.

No matter how much someone loves and cares for us, our hope must be rooted in God. By doing this we ensure that the balance of our lives is right. Too many people get married thinking that this person is the answer to all their problems. Their expectations of the other person, is too high, and so they are disappointed, and feel let down. God is the only one who never disappoints us.

Relationships are stunted when people, in effect, say "I'll love you, if you'll love me.!" Bob Mumford calls this, "Love with a hook!" A kind of boomerang love. The answer is to love unconditionally, like God loves us; seeking to serve and care for the other persons needs, instead of our own.

When both partners in a relationship do this, both find a great joy and delight in each other, as we have discovered! This time around our love is deeper, stronger; we are more sensitive of each other's needs and we have a much greater freedom to share our hearts with each other. There is a richness which has developed such as only comes with time. But then God kept promising Mike that ***"He would restore the years that the locust had eaten"!*** So we are not really surprised, just

To Have and To Hold

very thankful, for all that He has done in us and for us and through us!

Since our marriage there have been many times when we have had to give and take, as every other normal couple have to do. We didn't suddenly become Mr and Mrs perfectly suited, but what we did do was make the decision that this time we would see it through.

* * 🩷 * *

For our First Anniversary, we decided to go to Orlando, Florida and take all the family to Disney World for our first FAMILY holiday together in 19 years! We determined to make the most of the occasion!

Sitting here on the Florida sea shore, with the sun beating down, I can look backwards and forwards and with a grateful heart as I see for the first time, a family unit beginning to move together in unity.

As you read this story of the impossible becoming reality,

Remember!

All that you have read was only possible, by the Grace of Our Great and Mighty God.

* * 🩷 * *

**To be Continued to the End
Or until Jesus Returns for *His* Bride!**

Celia's Prologue

This is mainly for the benefit of those of you who are saying, "How did you stay so positive? Did you never have any doubts? The answer is, of course I had my doubts and no, I wasn't always positive.

In the early days, after Mike left me, I was incredulous that such a thing could have happened to us. I really hadn't realised that Mike was unhappy in our marriage... such was the breakdown in communication between us!

I was convinced that after a few weeks or months, Mike and I would be back together. However, I hadn't taken into account Mike's single-mindedness in pursuing a new love nor the sense of shame and loss of respect which he would have to face in order to return.

The first year in any bereavement is usually the hardest and so it was with me. I phoned my former Pastor, Reg and Nancy Taylor, to tell them of our split and Reg said, "She'll never marry again." These words haunted me down through the years, until Mike came back on the scene and I understood their meaning.

To Have and To Hold

I often felt that I wanted to break out of my situation, I watched as many of my friends moved away and started new lives, whilst I was hedged into my situation with no escape! I had made the decision that I wouldn't go looking for another husband, but that didn't mean that I didn't desire to be married or pray for the Lord to bring someone along! It just didn't happen.

I almost wished that I could start afresh with someone new rather than have to try to work through all the hurts of the past. The truth is, of course, that we all bring a certain amount of "baggage" into every relationship, so just the fact of having a different partner does not guarantee that things will work out any better!

Nor did I constantly pray for Mike, it was too painful, but there were times when the Lord brought him to mind and I would pray for him.

Of course, once he had returned to God like the Prodigal Son, and God had quickened my spirit to believe for restoration, I prayed believing that I already had the answer! I told many people that I believed our marriage would be restored and got very mixed reactions! Like "I wouldn't take my husband back!" "How could you do that?" "How can you forgive him for what he's done?"

Well, I had forgiven him years ago when he first left me, so where was the problem now? The embers of love were still burning they just needed to be fanned into life!

Sometimes, single people think that all their problems will vanish if they could only find the right partner. Married people can sometimes wish they were single again! What is the answer? The answer is in Jesus, He is the only one who can satisfy the deepest needs inside each of us, to be accepted for who we are, warts and all!

So we give all Praise and Honour and Glory to Jesus Christ, our Lord and King!

A Note on Restoration

In our modern day, Restoration means to return something to its former condition.

In Bible times there were laws pertaining to Restoration which required the person who had broken, stolen or otherwise deprived the owner of an item, not just to "make good" but to make better than when it was new.

This is what Pastor Malcolm spoke about in his address at our wedding. This is what we expected in our marriage and this is what has happened!

It was worth the wait, the hurts and the heartaches, it feels now as though we have always been together, our love is solid and strong and better than before.

I won't say I wouldn't change a thing; if I had a second chance, I'd like to think that maybe I would be more sensitive, more astute and wiser…but wisdom only comes through learning how to live though living and learning from our mistakes and those of others.

So, Yes!

If I had to choose, I'd do it all again!

Celia

Printed in the United Kingdom by
Lightning Source UK Ltd., Milton Keynes
139533UK00001B/19/A

9 781434 317438